Contents

Foreword

by Colin Bell, Chief Executive of Council of British International Schools (COBIS)

It has been a pleasure to write a foreword to this book, allowing me to reflect on my own early education. From a personal perspective, my earliest memories connected to my school years are vivid and fond. My prized, bright red tricycle was my treasured mode of transport to and from the Montessori playschool where my Mum was a teaching assistant. Together this trusty (all be it highly rickety) steed and I transported significant numbers of paintings, drawings, models, and what could loosely be classed as 'concept cookery' samples to and from home and playschool – my learning central.

Learning was always, fast, bright, textured, playful, varied and fun! Food colouring features heavily in my memory bank. I recall spending many a cherished afternoon adding colour drops to water contained in transparent plastic beakers to perform my own magic – with the finale act being to transfer water from different shaped beakers, cylindrical, rectangular and spherical, to another with the volume (bar natural spillages!), remaining largely intact. Great lifelong learning which has certainly helped me find order in the world despite not leading me to a coveted Nobel Peace Prize for special mechanics.

I remember too, a rich blend of music, rhyme, voices, song and laughter being the resounding sounds of my early years learning provision. Similar to resources found in quality settings today, displays were authentic, vibrant, eye catching, to serve purpose and to stimulate learning. Space, I recall was maximised to its potential. Displays hung, crept, grew and shrunk. Ones that morphed were always firm favourites.

Again, the things I remember were designated learning spaces; areas for PE, reading, role play, storytelling, painting, counting and fine art – more affectionately known as junk modelling. The smells I associate as an early learner include that of baking, play dough and freshly cut grass just before playtime. Perhaps you too share similar recollections?

As an early learner, being bestowed with a position of classroom responsibility was always something to be proud of, and something which would add a bound and a spring to one's step. Commander in Chief of Pencil Sharpening, Registrar of Registers, Director of Horticultural Irrigation Systems or what seemed often in my case, Head of Goldfish Nutrition was always a welcomed accolade.

My own training as an early year's teacher was a really valuable experience, which must have had a significant impact, enabling me to remember with saliency my own early learning. Since then I am fortunate to have enjoyed teaching across all ages in Asia, Europe and the UK. Through my training, I gained an understanding of why the teachers in my own playschool and primary school had such exceptionally well labelled cupboards, boxes and drawers. Everything had its place and there was a place for everything! Pair work, group work, individual work all supported by careful classroom management and meticulous planning. All sound familiar? These issues and more are covered in this book.

Working in the 'futures market' of high quality education is indeed a privilege, an honour and a constant learning experience. The precious commodities which together we nurture, grow and protect are of course the children, young people and families which we serve on a daily basis worldwide.

As early years practitioners, be you valued school leader, teacher, support staff or governor, you have every reason to be extremely proud of how your skills, expertise and experience provides solid lifelong learning foundations for highly inquisitive, enthusiastic and receptive young learners in a diverse range of educational settings.

Drawing upon talented experts in the field, the content of this inspirational book is practitioner led, with contributons from generous colleagues based in schools in Asia, Americas, Africa, Europe and The Middle East. The concept of the book is simple, yet powerful – to celebrate and highlight the creativity and excellence within early years education. All agreed and all aboard? Then, let our learning continue, develop and deepen...

Author biographies

Dr Anna Cox

Anna is the Programme Leader for a Postgraduate Certificate in Early Years Education (QTS) at the University of Northampton, where she is a Senior Lecturer in the School of Education. She is a Senior Fellow of the Higher Education Academy. Anna had extensive experience in a range of early years settings in the state and independent sectors before becoming a teacher educator. She is a passionate advocate of learning through play and supporting young children to be effective learners, which she shares with developing teachers through her role at the university and as an Early Years Consultant.

Gillian Sykes

Gillian is a Senior Lecturer in Education, and specialist in early years education at the University of Northampton. Her professional interests within the early years education field include: enabling environments; learning outdoors; the arts and creativity and supporting young children's writing development. She came to this role after being a specialist in the field of early years as a teacher, a lead teacher, a Forest School Practitioner, a mentor and Local Authority Early Years Senior Advisor. She supports early years teachers in 'communities of practice' through CPD projects alongside teaching on the BA QTS Early Years, PGCE QTS 3-7 and PGCE ITTEY 0-5 Programmes.

Dr Estelle Tarry

Estelle is a Senior Lecturer in Education at the University of Northampton and a Fellow of the Higher Education Academy. She teaches on undergraduate and postgraduate courses, including supporting international PhD students whose research focus is comparative education. Presently Estelle is the MA in Education (Full Time) Programme Leader. She has over 21 years teaching experience including 7 years as Head Teacher of international schools in Sri Lanka, Thailand and the Netherlands.

Eleonora Teszenyi

Eleonora is a Senior Lecturer in early years education at the University of Northampton. Before entering Higher Education she had worked in the early years sector for 19 years as a nursery practitioner, Early Years teacher/Early Years Professional, Early Years Advisor and Children Centre Teacher. Her specialist area is child development (birth to five years) and her current research projects include work on mixed and same-age groups in Hungarian kindergartens. Her other interests are related to parent partnerships and work-based learners in Higher Education.

Introduction

This book has been written by a small number of people who are passionate about the way that young children learn best. A shared view of the child at the centre of early learning binds the group and this holistic view informs the contents of all of the sections. In the 21st century what the future holds for young learners is unclear, what is clear is that they need to be confident, capable and resilient. As wider communication about education is increasing there is a developing understanding that children in settings across the globe learn in the same ways and have the same needs.

This book considers for the most part international and multicultural learning contexts. The term international school encompasses a wide range of schools catering for children of globally-mobile expatriates, 'host nationals' seeking an international advantage for their children, displaced national schools (*eg* American schools) and schools established for children of particular groups of employees (*eg* oil company schools). There are international groupings, such as United World Colleges (UWC), European Schools, English Schools Foundation (ESF) and more including 'state-funded' international schools (*eg* Dutch State International Primary Schools (Dips) and international school 'offspring' of 'mother schools' (*eg* Dulwich, Harrow and Haileybury). There are 'commercial enterprises' or 'family of schools' such as GEMS, Nord Anglia, Cognita, and Disney Schools of English in China. There are also some schools who are international by being affiliated nationally, regionally or by continent in some cases, to organisations such as Council of British International Schools (COBIS), European Council of International Schools (ECIS), Council of International Schools (COIS) or the Federation of British International Schools in South East Asia (FOBISSEA).

Multicultural contexts are those in which children from a range of cultural, national and/or linguistic backgrounds learn and play together. These can be national state provision as well as international schools. Increasing global mobility is leading to more multicultural contexts for learning across Europe and beyond. There is, at the same time, an increasing growth in the availability of international programmes such as Primary Years Programme (PYP) and International Primary Curriculum (IPC) taught in multicultural contexts. Global dimensions of education in the United Kingdom schools are shaped by government strategies such as the 'Prevent Strategy' (TSO, 2012) and the new National Curriculum (Department of Education, 2013). Citizenship education can and often does provide a home for global issues within the curriculum and for younger children this happens through personal, social and emotional development and through learning about communities as they gain an understanding of the world.

This means that international and/or multicultural contexts will be part of the career experience of many teachers whether they themselves are mobile or not. Teacher training is now being undertaken by a more varied participant group, and this is a great bonus to the profession. The contribution to children's learning that results from being taught by a range of teachers with different nationalities, cultural, language and religious backgrounds is considerable. So this book celebrates diversity among early years teachers and aims to encourage them to share some features of heritage, nationality or religion and their particular blend of experiences with the children they teach. This is not to invite proselytising or imperialism but to celebrate the variety amongst teachers as well as that among the children that they teach.

This book is not curriculum led but sets out to consider and explore some important features of effective practice in educating young children. Teachers, like families and carers seek to enable children to gain the skills, knowledge and understanding that will help them become confident members of society, wherever in the world they are. Supporting children to be confident learners, to question what they see and hear and to think for themselves is critical and play provides a mechanism for just this kind of development. Play can happen as children explore resources provided by their teachers, as they find their way around environments created by their teachers and as they solve problems set by their teachers. Play is not incidental nor without intention from the teacher who provided the opportunities but this is not always recognised outside the early years education community.

Some would argue that at this time early years teachers are under downward pressure from colleagues who teach older children. Some teachers of older children feel that early years teachers provide *only* the starting blocks for the education *they* deliver as children progress through the school system. This influence, perceived or real, may go some way to explain the UK curriculum for young learners being called the Early Years Foundation Stage (DfE, 2014). However this is far from the whole picture and for many early years teachers this does not reflect their strongly held and well informed beliefs about how young children learn as well as how and what they are best taught. The EYFS and other early education programmes may more optimistically be seen as creating the very bedrock on which other learning is founded, and to which it continues to be bound. The UK international school case study demonstrates how later learning is founded, including in the outdoors, on skills and knowledge developed in the early years. Bruner (1963) notes that mathematics or history are not taught to create little libraries of mathematics or history but to help children think mathematically or to consider issues as a historian does. The underpinnings of this kind of learning come through the early experiences of children. For example as they begin to make choices in their play and developing critical skills and as they respond to experiences from their play through representative actions and talk, they are building a repertoire of ways to understand the world.

Effective practice in early years education at the start of the 21st century is informed by secure pedagogical models. These are specific to the skills and abilities of young children as well as meeting their learning and development needs. Children's experiences of the world vary but the direct engagement that they enjoy as they learn is not nationally or regionally situated. However, children cannot all be taught in the same way and some of the reasons for this are illustrated in the case study section of this book. Early years teachers need to have ownership of the ways of working that best meet the needs of those they teach and find ways into their children's learning. They must teach in ways which are in tune with the children's cultural approach to learning, the confidence that they have in their own learning and the cultural capital that they share (or not) with the dominant learning culture of the school or setting.

Purpose and rationale of book

This book sets out to help people passionate about high quality provision for young learners to be able to

- Justify their pedagogy and practice to others
- Access and consider a range of perspectives on what 'good practice' looks like
- Access a range of research and references if they want to widen their knowledge
- Engage in further reflection on their own practice.

Not least the authors hope that readers will be enthused and excited by the range of case studies alongside the more formal chapters at the start of the book.

Who is this book for?

This book is for early years teachers, phase leaders, junior school Headteachers and others interested in high quality education for the youngest children. Trainee teachers will also find this book valuable in broadening their perspectives of children's learning in international and multicultural contexts. School governors with an interest in young learners may enjoy this book too.

What is the book all about?

The five chapters of this book cover a range of contemporary issues in early years education in international and/or multicultural contexts. Chapters are written by specialists in early years education in the UK and internationally. Chapter 1 describes some of the historical influences on current understandings how young children (those aged from birth to three and from three to seven years) are educated in the 21st century, it considers play and playful pedagogy and aims to set the scene for Chapters 2 to 5.

In Chapter 2 the critical role of the adult is examined, taking account of children's physical, emotional and intellectual development. The notion of professional love in teaching young children is also presented in that chapter. The connections between schools and parents are examined in Chapter 3, across a range of contexts. The chapter offers a range of views about working with parents and carers derived from a number of different national settings and goes on to offer suggestions about good practice. Chapter 4 is dedicated to the importance of environments for learning, and how they impact on different children and their learning. The final chapter, Chapter 5 is about learning outdoors, and includes risk management by adults and the importance of children taking risks in their play. It also describes some of the many benefits of learning outdoors.

The later chapter of the book consists of nine case studies, but before these is a picture section in which some aspects of practice in the participating settings are shared. The case studies follow and they come from Netherlands, Italy, Uganda, Qatar, Romania, Mexico, Indonesia and the United Kingdom. Each has focused on an aspect of their practice and they include: creating an appropriate learning environment, outdoor free flow play, engaging with parents and careers, planning and assessment for learning, play as learning, supporting the curriculum for young learners, moving beyond the outdoor classroom, and what teaching looks like in the early years. The final case study offers links to the education of children beyond the early years but has many resonances with the chapter on learning outdoors. It provides a useful reminder that good practice in early years and good practice in other stages of education are not unconnected. Through the main chapter links to the case studies are made. Readers will find many more links for themselves.

This book came about because a very diverse group of people had the opportunity to share their ideas about effective practice in the early years – its joys and its challenges. Reflecting on our own practice and practice we have observed has stimulated the writing. If it stimulates early years teachers to reflect on their practice too and on the privilege of working with young children, the authors will be very happy.

References

Bruner, J. (1963) *The process of education.* Cambridge, MA: Harvard University Press

The Stationery Office (2012) *Prevent Strategy.* London: TSO

DfE (2014) *Statutory framework for the early years foundation stage.* Runcorn: Department for Education

www.gov.uk/government/publications/early-years-foundation-stage-framework--2

(accessed 31st March 2015)

Chapter 1

Overlapping arenas of knowledge informing early years education

by Anna Cox

This chapter considers some of the historical influences on how young children (those aged from birth to three and from three to seven years) are educated in the 21st century. The chapter contains ideas from a range of disciplines but certainly does not cover all that informs high quality early years experiences. It aims to set the scene for the more specific chapters which follow, so many themes are introduced which are expanded elsewhere. Chapter 2 discusses play as a means of learning and what playful learning means. These two chapters support the rest of the book.

As mentioned in the introduction, some would argue that at this time early years' teachers are under downward pressure from colleagues who teach older children. It is sometimes the case that those teaching older children view early years' teachers as providing the starting blocks for the education *they* will deliver as children progress through the school system. The notion of setting children off on a secure path to later learning is not a bad one, but to think of the role of early years teachers as only this is hard to accept. It can result in an influence, perceived or real, that the role of the early years teacher is to get children ready for 'real' school. However this is far from the view of most early years teachers, for them this preparation-ist view does not reflect their strongly held and well informed beliefs about how young children learn, nor how and what they are best taught. The role of the early years teacher is to prepare children for life not simply for formal schooling. To provide young learners with opportunities to learn in their own ways and through artefacts and resources that stimulate their interest is a positive interpretation of the 'Early Years Foundation Stage' (Early Education, 2012) which is the guidance under which children under five are educated in the United Kingdom.

In contrast to any sense of downward pressure or meeting the needs of other phases of education, this book is founded on the belief that effective practice in early years education at the start of the 21st century is informed by secure pedagogical models. Also that these are specific to the skills and abilities of young children, as well as meeting their learning and development needs. Children's experiences of the world vary but the direct engagement that they enjoy as they learn is not nationally or regionally situated.

The ways that young children learn best is more fully understood today than they have ever been. Ways of supporting the learning of young children are notable for being holistic, taking account of the whole child not just their intellectual development. The degree to which differentiation allows teachers to meet children's learning and welfare needs is well expressed in the early years classroom. Knowing about children is the fundamental binding principle that holds together the range of theorists and thinkers who have contributed to current understandings. Starting with the child is a recurring theme in contemporary practice and is a key feature of the philosophy of education among early years teachers. This notion did not arise spontaneously; it is informed by great thinkers of the past such as John Amos Comenius, John Locke and Jean Jacques Rousseau. These pioneers held views of the child that noted individuality and the capacity to learn and develop. Rousseau valued the outdoor environment for learning and this remains a feature of effective early years practice almost universally. It manifests in different ways in the 21st century, for example through 'Forest Schools' from Scandinavia and the development of 'outdoor classrooms' which attract and support both the most active children and those who are less outgoing and who enjoy solitude in the open. More about learning in the outdoor appears in both Chapter 5 and in case studies in Chapter 7. They note that climate and location impact the capacity of international settings to offer outdoor provision as well as some of the factors that must be taken into account to do so. This is clear in the Indonesia case study in particular.

The overarching ideas that support early years practice come from other pioneers too, such as Johann Heinrich Pestallozzi and Friedrich Froebel. Froebel was a strong proponent of the view that women could be teachers, a notion not favoured by earlier thinkers nor by many of his contemporaries. In most early years classrooms today, practice is led by women, and in the United Kingdom there is a recognised need to bring more men into primary (5-11 years) if not early years (three - seven years) education (Faulstich-Wieland, 2013). Data from the World Bank (2014) indicates that in many nations women teachers significantly outnumber men teachers in Primary education in the 21st century. Some potential reasons for this are interesting to consider. Perhaps there is a perception that young children relate to females who are in some sense 'standing in' for their mothers (this idea is clearly challenged in Chapter 2 where the notion of a secondary care giver is discussed). It may be because the potential of staff from early years gaining career progression is seen to be less. Statistics were not found to substantiate this but anecdotal evidence from both UK and international colleagues lent some weight to the argument. Some still consider early years teaching is really 'baby-sitting' and that early years teachers play all day in the sand - this holds back its status and can reduce the confidence of individual early years teachers. This misguided view is still heard and is not likely to make an early years role very attractive despite that view being misplaced! There may be additional reasons for this to do with culture and religion which may play a part, and which should be respected alongside being challenged when this can be done respectfully.

Going back to the pioneers, Friedrich Froebel (1782 - 1852) linked in his naming of kindergarten the ideas of gardens of children and gardens for children expanding on the ideas of Rousseau and others. Froebel (1782 - 1852) is recognised for *his* 'kindergarten' settings, the use of the term garden communicating not only outdoor learning but the nurture of the child as a plant is nurtured in the garden. His ideas were adopted in Europe and beyond and are still very influential. Most training for early years teachers in the UK and Europe will include a consideration of Froebel's work (as well as that of a selection of other pioneers). Froebel's terminology reflects that respect that he had for the child. His description of his carefully designed learning resources as 'gifts' indicates the value that he attributed to supporting children's learning and the sequential nature of the 'gifts' demonstrates an understanding and respect for the construction of knowledge.

Similarly the work of Maria Montessori is generally well known to early years teachers and there is a well-established movement internationally providing Montessori education. The Montessori pedagogical approach supports children to learn and develop as individuals. They are encouraged by adults to gain in confidence and independence, to enable them to develop socially and academically. Montessori settings have a particular ethos and they (as many others) value and support partnership with parents and carers, a topic discussed in Chapter 3. The nature of resources used in Montessori settings is recognised to be very important to the learning. Children are encouraged to undertake exercises in daily living, that is to say children learn movements and activities which are universal like pouring, folding and carrying and self-care like hand washing. The recent popularity of the 'dough disco' or 'dough gym' in which children manipulate play dough to music shows how teachers in other contemporary settings supporting the same development of dexterity within their own ethos and approach. Furthermore a whole range of independence skills feature in other contemporary contexts as well as Montessori education and are a recognised part of 21st century early years education in a wide range of schools and settings.

Similar themes and values have been explored by more recent thinkers such as Jean Piaget, Erik Erikson and others. Increasingly early years practice is informed by research and by reflection on research alongside reflection on practice. The constructivist theory of Piaget, seeing children as lone scientists is a strong influence on early years practice along with theories of the social construction of knowledge arising from the work of Vygotsky. Reflective early years teachers value and provide for children to experiment and find out for themselves. They do this, for example, in free play with malleable materials or activities which support other aspects of expressive arts and design. They also provide for children to develop their thinking through dialogue with others using strategies such as 'think, pair, share' and 'talk partners' to promote learning from peers and through sustained shared thinking. Sustained shared thinking came to the knowledge of practitioners following The Effective Provision of Pre-school Education (EPPE) project, in which it was recognised that interactions between children and adults impacted on thinking skills and cognitive development. Sylva, Siraj-Blatchford, Taggart, Sammons, Elliot, and Melhuish (2004) noted that when children had been supported in their thinking by supportive adults they did better than those whose thinking had been done alone or only with other children. This was indeed a highly significant finding for early years practitioners, linking social constructivism and established effective practice. Robson, writing about children's creative thinking (2012:31) suggests that 'the creation of an atmosphere in which children are encouraged to reflect on their thinking, may be most important.' It was observed that effective sustained shared thinking episodes were usually initiated by a child or children and then sustained through skilful interactions by the adult. The fact the EPPE work was carried out in pre-school settings does nothing to detract from its importance in highlighting that early years teachers, trained for this key role, and other classroom adults are crucial resources. The role of adults is further discussed in Chapter 2.

The most contemporary influence on reflective early years teachers is that of neuroscience. Knowledge of the developing brain has significantly increased in the past 30 years, with the Centre for Neuroscience in Education being established at Cambridge University (UK) in 2005. A range of applications of neuroscientific understandings are available for teachers, for example Nath and Szűcs (2014) explain the value of construction play in supporting mathematical development.

It is known that the physical structures of the brain are formed before birth and that though specific areas of the brain have particular functions they work in networks or collections of areas to enable the brain to function. During childhood brain areas related to language, memory, attention and emotions develop. As children's brains gradually mature they gain greater capacity for planned action, the role of the early years teacher is to be responsive to this through their interactions with children and the environment they provide. Parents and those working with young children know that there are times when learning leaps ahead and times of consolidation. Brain scanning technologies have shed light on these sensitive periods and on the way that young brains work. A child's body at rest does not indicate a brain at rest. Perhaps most interesting to early years teachers is the development of the child's social brain, relating to the strong sense of security and belonging described in Chapter 2. The impact of deprivation on learning and development in young children is also now more widely understood; neglect, maltreatment or abuse are known to affect the young brain. However, less extreme issues also affect children so allowing sleepy children some time to rest in a cosy place in the class is sometimes the appropriate response. The value of cosy spaces is further explored in Chapter 4.

Neurophysiological research is increasingly relevant to issues such as reading and writing acquisition, to memory and learning, and metacognition in young children. Flavell (1987) suggested that children could and should learn about their own learning. He identifies three areas which support young learners: having an awareness of knowledge (knowing what they know); having an awareness of thinking (knowing that they can solve problems) and an awareness of thinking strategies (knowing ways to start to solve problems). *How do early years teachers help this important development?* Strategies include: modelling thinking out loud for children, in line with principles of sustained shared thinking (Tinzmann, 1990); scaffolding thinking, in line with the work of Bruner (1978) and Vygotsky (1978); and identifying opportunities for thinking, seen clearly in the Building Learning Power programme of Claxton (2002).

Interestingly a binding principle informs all of the thinkers and the theories explored in this chapter, and that is that the way in which we teach young children must be based on an understanding of their needs, interests and abilities as they grow and mature. The importance of a secure understanding of child development in its broadest sense is now recognised to be crucial to effective practice (Nutbrown, 2012). This links well to the finding of neuroscience that children's development has a passage through sensitive periods of learning. The developmental stages described by Piaget are now seen to be much more flexible and overlapping than they once were and the importance of environmental factors is known to impact children's capacity to learn (Nutbrown, 2006).

Good early years teachers know the children that they teach and are able to respond to this. This represents a major shift in thinking away from a view that large groups or classes of young children could be taught the same thing at the same time in the same way.

One of the ways that this differentiated approach was captured in the United Kingdom is through the themes of the first Early Years Foundation Stage (DfE, 2008) documentation. This presented four themes to underpin practice, one of which was 'Unique Child'. This migrated to become one of the four guiding principles of the 2014 version of the framework (DfE, 2014). It is stated in that document that 'every child is a unique child, who is constantly learning and can be resilient, capable, confident and self-assured'. That children can display these capacities is not doubted by informed and committed early years teachers and effective pedagogy reflects this.

In addition to the thinking of pioneers in the education of young children the United Nations Convention on the Rights of the Child (UN General Assembly, 1989) underpins, directly or indirectly, much of what is explored in this book. Historically it marks a turning point in taking to a global audience the ways in which children should be supported on their journey to adulthood. Early years teachers help to set the youngest children on this journey and to develop the knowledge, skills and attitudes which will make them effective learners throughout their life course. The adoption of the Convention has been slower in some nations than others but it is the most widely ratified Human Rights treaty in history. It is ratified in 192 nations with Somalia unable to ratify because of lack of stable government and the United States indicating its intention to ratify but not having done so. So the treaty is in the frame of reference for educators across the globe. It is embedded in educational practice with children from three to seven to different degrees and with different levels of ownership by early years teachers across the globe. Well informed and reflective teachers not only acknowledge the themes of the convention but use it to shape their practice in the classroom.

Early years teachers as a professional group need to be and generally are reflective, so that as part of the role that they hold they have a state of mind or way of being that allows them to learn from their own practice. Reflection is not an add-on or a task to be completed at the end of a lesson or activity. Reflection enables early years teachers to challenge their own and others assumptions about children, about learning and about teaching. The development of a personal pedagogy is often the result of such reflection and can result in a very personal philosophy of education. Beyond being reflective it is important for early years teachers to be reflexive, and that is a harder concept to capture in this summary. Reflexive early years teachers look within themselves and respond to their experiences, act as researchers into their practice and taking account of how they impact the situations they are considering. Reflective practice and reflexivity are ways of being, an ongoing integral part of practice, not a technique, or requirement. It is useful to consider them as a pedagogical approach. They are what Fanghanel (2004: 576) called 'the pearl grit in the oyster of practice and education'. Sharing the grit and the pearls with others to build communities of practice is very important for both personal and professional practice.

Early years practice and pedagogy is both culturally and historically specific across the world, and only some of the ways that this manifests can be shared here. We do indeed 'stand on the shoulders of giants' some of whom are mentioned earlier in this chapter, but the practice that is developed in each context has to feel right for everyone involved: each child, each family, each professional. One particular approach, or example of good practice, cannot be transported from one context to another without adjustments: the same way as a flower cannot be uprooted from one soil and planted in another and expected to flourish the same way. Awareness of this specificity, along with a sound understanding of child development should be the guiding light in providing the best possible start for children's life-long learning. But even this is to be considered with a great degree of flexibility: depending on children's adjustment and adaptation to life experiences and their uneven and very individual pace of development and learning.

References

Bruner, J. S. (1978) The role of dialogue in language acquisition. In A. Sinclair, R., J. Jarvelle, and W. J.M. Levelt (Eds) *The Child's Concept of Language*. New York: Springer-Verlag

Claxton, G. (2002) *Building Learning Power*. Bristol: TLO Ltd

DfE (2012) *Statutory framework for the early years foundation stage*. Department for Education: Runcorn

DfE (2014) *Statutory framework for the early years foundation stage*. Department for Education: Runcorn

Fanghanel, J. (2004) *Capturing dissonance in university teacher education environments*. Studies in Higher Education, 29(5), 575–90

Faulstich-Wieland, H. (2013) *Should male primary school teachers be there principally as role models for Boys?* Universal Journal of Educational Research 1(2), 65-73

Flavell, J. H. (1987) Speculation about the nature and development of metacognition. In F. Weinert & R. Kluwe (Eds.) *Metacognition, motivation, and understanding*, 21 - 29. Hillsdale, NJ: Lawrence Erlbaum

Nath S & Szűcs D (2014) *Construction play and cognitive skills associated with the development of mathematical abilities in 7-year-old children*. Learning and Instruction, 32, 73-80

Nutbrown, C. (2006) *Threads of thinking: young children learning and the role of early education* (3rd edn). London: Sage

Nutbrown, C. (2012) *Foundations for quality: The independent review of early education and childcare qualifications, Final Report*. Department for Education: Runcorn

Robson, S. (2012) 'Creative thinking in early childhood' in Fumoto, H., Robson, S., Greenfield,

S., and Hargreaves, D., (Eds) *Young children's creative thinking*, 27 -40. *London*: Sage

Sylva, K., Siraj-Blatchford, I., Taggart, B., Sammons, P., Elliot, K., and Melhuish, E., (2004) *The Effective Provision of Preschool Education (EPPE) Project Technical Paper 12 – The Final* Report: Effective Preschool Education. London: DfES and Institute of Education, University of London

Tinzmann, M.B., Jones, B.F., Fennimore, T.F., Bakker, J., Fine, C., and Pierce, J. (1990) *What is the collaborative classroom?* North Central Regional Educational Laboratory. Oak Brook. Available at http://www.ncrel.org/sdrs/areas/rpl_esys/collab.html [1Accessed 1st April 2015]

UN General Assembly, *Convention on the Rights of the Child*, 20 November 1989, United Nations, Treaty Series, 1577, 3, available at: http://www.refworld.org/docid/3ae6b38f0.html [Accessed 1st April 2015]

Vygotsky, L. S. (1978) *Mind in society: The development of higher psychological processes*. Cambridge, MA: Harvard University Press

World Bank (2014) Primary Education, Teachers, % Female [on-line] Available: http://data.worldbank.org/indicator/SE.PRM.TCHR.FE.ZS [Accessed 17th February 2015]

Chapter 2

Play and playful learning

by Anna Cox and Eleonora Teszenyi

When the word play is used its meaning is perceived differently by different audiences. Even among educators there is a diversity of understanding. It is not unusual to hear play contrasted with 'work' in primary classrooms and play is seldom mentioned in secondary classrooms. In early years education play has a very different meaning, which does not contrast it with work but recognises it as work. For children, especially young children, play is the work of learning. But this valued perspective of play does not mean football club, dance classes or horse riding but child initiated play in which exploration, problem-solving and imagining happen. These activities, undertaken alone, or with peers or adults, enables young minds to grow connections which help them understand the world they live in.

It is worth noting that some theories separate work and play and others consider the two as one. This presents a dilemma in discussing play which has not been resolved, and indeed may not be. Recreation theory sees a distinction between play and learning. It views play as trivial and something that is done after work as relaxation. This view seems to underpin some conversations between early years teachers and parents and carers; particularly when children are asked what they have done at school today they reply 'nothing, we played all day'. The value of play then needs to be shared with parents, to enable them to see the important learning that is taking place through what is lightly labelled play. Recreation theory (Mitchell and Mason, 1948) is not helpful in understanding the significance of play in children's learning and development! Its origins may come from Spencer's (1872) excess energy theory, viewing play as letting off steam and play for self-gratification, without a purpose. Such a view is not widely held today.

Theories connecting play and learning also have history. This comes from, for example Hall's recapitulation theory (described in Curtis, 1916: 5). Play is seen as having a significance in linking children to the past, not just past generations but past ages. This view suggests that when children play they are enacting behaviours that reflect the evolutionary past. Children are seen to be behaving instinctively; den building, fire making rituals or imagined weapons reflect a primitive past. Part of this group of theory is the work of Groos (1901: 361 - 406) whose practice theory states that childhood is a stage of dependence and *exists* for play – play helps children to prepare for adult life by letting them practice and explore adult roles in a natural way. Clearly play is important for children and so important also to the adults who work with them.

This is recognised in the United Nations Convention on the Rights of the Child (UN General Assembly, 1989) which states in Article 31 that **"The child has the right to** leisure, **play** and participation in cultural and artistic activities". Where play is both a right and a means of learning its importance cannot be doubted. Sometimes though, it is challenged – some adults do not attach importance to play because they hold a very narrow concept of play. They think play is only for children's recreation or they are unaware of the developmental value of play and so they think it is unimportant and should not be part of education. This chapter tries to explore the importance of play and of playful learning as crucial learning for young children, and very much at the heart of education. Paley (2005) reiterates play is children's work. She goes on to say that she fears that in some practice this is not valued and 'work' is in fact presented to children as play. This claimed 'play' is instructional in nature, out-of context and not organic to children but is sometimes being presented as play. It is her belief and one shared by the authors of this book that children are intended to play and that they play with ideas to make sense of the complex world around them.

Sitting alongside the earlier discussion, what play is remains contested. Simple means of defining play are typographies which dissect play into a series of categories. One of the most well know of these is that of Parten (1932). The way in which she approaches defining play is through the development and nature of children's participation. An adapted version of her typography follows:

Unoccupied play - when a child is not actively playing but watching things that happen to catch his interest. The child may play with his own fingers or limbs, move around, remain in one location, or follow a teacher.

Onlooker behaviour - this stage is called behaviour rather than play because such a child is content watching other children.

Solitary independent play – when children prefer to play by themselves and do not comfortably interact with other children. They may play at a distance with favourite, chosen toys. They are often in listening distance of other but show little interest in making contact. When contact happens it may take the form of grabbing other children's toys opportunistically.

Parallel play – this is sometimes called adjacent play or social co-action. Children occupy space near others, but do not often share toys or materials. They may be heard to be speaking but not to one another. Each has their own conversation and there is no attempt to communicate. As a result unconnected conversations can be overheard.

Associative play – in this play children lend, borrow, and take toys from one another. However, it's not co-operative and so a culture exists of "every one for himself." Children are beginning to engage in close personal contact but they still consider their own viewpoint as most important. They are not yet ready to participate in teams or group work, but providing opportunities to function as a team help them to gradually learn how to communicate their needs.

Co-operative play – this is said by Parten (1932) to be the highest form of children working and playing together. They engage in behaviours valued by adults such as sharing, taking turns, and undertaking or responding to leadership for the group. In cooperative play it is noted that three-year-olds play best with approximately three other children while five-year-olds can play successfully with approximately five children.

Parten also found that as children became older and with more opportunities for peer interaction, the non-social types (solitary and parallel) declined in favour of the social types. In international and multicultural settings reflecting on these categories can give an indication of where in their play development children are and perhaps provide a guide to what play opportunities or experiences a child joining the group may have had.

Thinking more simply, play is considered by some to be natural and spontaneous to children; for example babies make free body movements, sounds and responses to adults who care for them. This is seen as early play. As children grow, their spontaneous play sometimes becomes more organised and activity oriented. They enjoy and develop through running, jumping and other gross motor movements. Fine movements develop through manipulation of objects. Child development is well understood by adults or at least information about it is accessible to them, for example from health professionals or from the many books on the subject (Robinson 2008; Lindon 2012; Spock and Needlman 2012).

In Chapter 1 a number of early childhood pioneers who have shaped our view of children and how they play, learn and develop were mentioned. Comenius was on that list and is one of the earlier 'giants'. In his 'Didactica Magna' of 1638 he associated teacher instruction with 'useless labour' in the classroom and promotes enjoyable, playful learning experiences that result in 'solid progress'. This playful learning links to one of the three child/adult and teaching/learning models described in Chapter 3. The interactionist model recognises the value of child initiated play and sees children and adults as co-players. This play by which children unify experience links strongly to playful pedagogies. In contrast to this and at the other end of a continuum is the empiricist model where play (if it can rightly be called that) is controlled by the adults. This view does not sit well with the authors of this book and is not a prominent view of play in the 21st century. Sitting between these two is the psycho-analytic view of play: play to manage feelings (and linked to the seminal works of Freud, Erikson, Winnicott). In teaching young children the middle ground of this continuum is fertile territory, but the balance can shift. Learning through play remains a complex concept.

Positive play experiences develop positive emotional well-being. Children's mastery of both objects and ideas in play supports self-belief and confidence. Many, such as Claxton (2005), recognise the value of failure and unresolved challenge in play. This supports the development of resilience and perseverance which will help children in their later learning and in the challenges that adult life will throw at them. Play has great potential to help children gain confidence to keep trying when things do not go to plan, a much easier lesson to learn during den making than meeting it first in a formal academic situation. Similarly problem solving skills resulting from challenging play can be lessons for life.

As mentioned earlier play is seen differently by children and adults; whether those adults are educators or parents and carers. It could be said that adults are busy working a lot of the time and they take part in play for recreation. This might be visiting the cinema, reading a book or sharing a meal with friends as well as many other things. Adults' view of their play is often in contrast to work. Children play more freely and it is this playfulness that effective early learning can be based on. Broadhead and Burt (2012) set out to help early years teachers and practitioners understand what playful learning means and they use the term 'playful pedagogies' to do this. They explain pedagogy as what adults do to provide learning and teaching experiences and they go on to add that it is informed by teachers and practitioners own understanding of why they do what they do (Broadhead and Burt, 2012). Playful pedagogies access the dispositions of children to play and build on them to support effective learning. Not all learning happens through child initiated play, though effective early years teachers resource their learning environments for much of this to take place and this is described in Chapter 4. Ways in which children's needs are met through child initiated play are diverse, and this is particularly the case in multicultural and international settings. The case studies reveal some of these differences, as well as the constraints that impact on particular settings and the opportunities too. As a means of considering the opportunities to be a successful, playful learner it is useful to look at some attributes of learning. The following list of attributes or dispositions to learning came from interviews of pupils, head teachers in schools and national policy makers about what makes an effective learner (Claxton, 2007: 117). Effective learners are capable of being:

- Curious, adventurous and questioning
- Resilient, determined and focused

- Open minded, flexible, imaginative and creative
- Critical, sceptical and analytical
- Both methodical and opportunistic
- Reflective, thoughtful and self-evaluative
- Keen to build on their products and performances
- Collaborative but also independent.

This list might seem full of contradictions or at least dichotomies, such as the combination of flexible and focused or of determined and open-minded. It can also be a catalyst for questioning and reflection on practice that supports effective and playful learning. Are collections of interesting objects part of the setting resources? They might be shells, boxes or small world characters, for example. These justify their play in several ways: as flexible play prompts being treasures in their own right and as objects which encourage methodical organisation and analysis by young learners. Obscure objects like single shoes which appear overnight in the setting encourage reflection and questioning, imagination and performances. There is little doubt that such learning opportunities are playful, and playful practitioners will enjoy them as much as the children. Sharing pleasure and excitement with young children is one of the joys of the job of being an early years teacher. Helping young children to construct their knowledge of the world is not an information sharing exercise, it should be a journey travelled together.

Bringing together the characteristics of effective learning for young children and the characteristics of play opens a door to different kinds of practice. That is the playful pedagogies that this book supports. So what are playful pedagogies? There is no list to consult or manual to follow but there are some good signposts for practitioners to follow. Like the elephant to the blindfolded man, with a little careful exploring you should be able to recognise it when you have found it! Isaacs (1971) saw play as essential to learning but also felt that adults should see the child's view through undertaking observation to inform practice. This is certainly true of playful pedagogies, which need to arise from the children's knowledge, interests and experiences as they manifest themselves in the setting. It cannot be forgotten that play is a culturally located notion, and so in international and multicultural settings children's and families' views of play may differ from that of the dominant culture of the school or setting.

This is supported by the view of Vygotsky that play is not necessarily a natural phenomenon that comes only from children's instinctive 'playful' tendencies. The degree to which adults engage with children and the way they do this can mediate the children's activities. The interventions may be socially important, perhaps curbing excesses and ensuring care for others. In contrast to this adult mediation may be restrictive; anxious and risk averse teachers are unlikely to encourage children to play boldly. So though adult engagement is important it can shape the play that is seen in a particular cultural context (Bodrova, 2008: 359).

Shaping playful pedagogies is not the easiest way to work with young children but it might prove to be the most effective for your community of practice. It can be a developmental approach to creating the best setting possible for the children who attend. Even this simple statement indicates the need for constant change in international and multicultural settings, as in any others. Children and families connected to the setting will change quickly so rapid communication with new families, adaptions of resources for previously unfamiliar cultures and languages, the building of sensitive relationships with individual children, the nurturing of supportive relationships between children and working respectfully with them are all important. Those are bones for playful pedagogy but the meat of it is something more.

Playful pedagogy in practice does not have a checklist of features but there are pointers that things are moving in the right direction. The journey is not one with a final destination because the best of practice continues to evolve and change to meet needs. The pointers that playful pedagogy is being developed can include:

- ✓ An environment in which all kinds of play are equally valued, there is no hierarchy of worth
- ✓ Authentic experiences are provided for children for them to extrapolate in their play
- ✓ Teachers value their role as play partners as well as leading learning in more orthodox ways
- ✓ Children's responses to activities provided are respected and opportunities provided to develop their interests in ways that promote deep level learning not 'replication with variation'
- ✓ Activities are not set up to test what children can or cannot do, but

assessment of children's attainment and progress is understood, recorded and shared with parents and carers alongside sharing the children's interest in learning

✓ Making activities playful is valued but this is done in response to children's cultural interests and intellectual interests

✓ Physicality in play and learning is valued in both boys and girls, and communication through body language, proximity and physical contact between children is also valued

✓ Children are allowed to occupy a wide emotional range, they are not constricted by having to be 'happy' all the time, emotions are respected

✓ There is lots of laughing, children and their teachers have fun

✓ Children and adults relish laughter and fun, and they enjoy one another's company

✓ Some play opportunities are prolonged and returned to by the children, and they are not made to 'move on' in line with an adult directed schedule

✓ It is understood that building knowledge comes from being part of a learning community with others, some like yourself and others not

Practitioners will find many other keys to playful pedagogy in their own practice. In international and multicultural settings some awareness of particular challenges must be acknowledged. For example, where all kinds of play are valued parental responses will vary, so the strong relationship between parents and settings described later in this book are very significant. Equally it is possible that a shared vision of what play is and what play means may dominate in a setting. The result of this can be to put unspoken barriers in the way of children's play development, so team reflection and negotiation of shared meaning when discussing play is very important. No one definition of play is universally held and so the values and beliefs of teachers in settings and classrooms shape it contextually. Sometimes this means that personal views (or perhaps prejudices) about children and childhood could over-run more professional thinking. Having something to hang conversations and reflections about play onto can be really helpful in this situation. Hughes (2001) wrote that play has two interlinked characteristics which are i) that it has an immediate impact for the players and helps them make sense of their situation and place in the world and ii) that play has a wider nature beyond the impact on individual players and is built into a child's personal history. That is to say that the individual child players will make meaning from the experience not just learn from it. This can only happen through real, authentic experiences, for example children seeing building going on at a next door plot and going on to make buildings and machines with the resources and materials available to them.

Children's play has fascinated educators, child psychologists, and scientists for centuries. Scholer (2001) who is a paediatrician at Vanderbilt University in the USA and who created 'Play Nicely' (a programme for supporting parents to understand and support children's behaviour) says, "One reason for the interest in play among theorist is that through play children learn to be creative and use their imagination". What children learn best is what they learn through play, so play should be the universally acknowledged and legitimate method of teaching during the child's early years. It is not yet but perhaps one day it will be. Then the view of Chazan will be more widely heard.

'Playing and growing are synonymous with life itself. Playfulness bespeaks creativity and action, change and possibility of transformation. Play activity thus reflects the very existence of the self, that part of the organism that exists both independently and interdependently, that can reflect upon itself and be aware of its own existence. In being playful the child attains a degree of autonomy sustained by representations of his inner and outer worlds'. (2002:198)

References

Bodrova, E. (2008) *Make believe play versus academic skills: A Vygotskyan approach to today's dilemma of early childhood education.* European Early Childhood Research Journal, 16 (3) 357 - 369

Broadhead, B. and Burt, A. (2012) *Understanding young children's learning through play: Building playful pedagogies.* Abingdon: Routledge

Chazan, S. (2002) *Profiles of play: Assessing and observing structure and process in play therapy.* London: Jessica Kingsley Publishers

Claxton, G. (2007) Expanding young people's capacity to learn. *British Journal of Educational Studies,* 55 (2) 115 – 134

Hughes, B. (2002) *Playworker's taxonomy of play types* (2nd Ed). London: PlayLink

Groos, K. (1901) *The play of man,* translated by Elizabeth L. Baldwin. New York: Appleton

Isaacs, S. (1971) *The nursery years: The mind of the children from birth to six years.* London: Routledge

Lindon, J. (2012) *Understanding child development: 0 to 8 years.* London: Hodder Education

Mitchell, E. D. and Mason, B. S. (1948) *The theory of play.* New York: A.S. Barnes

Paley, V. G. (2005) *A child's work.* Chicago: University of Chicago Press

Robinson, M. (2008) *Child development from birth to eight.* Maidenhead: Open University Press

Scholer, S. (2001) *Play nicely: Recommendations for managing aggression in young children.* Nashville, Tennessee: Vanderbilt Press

Spock, B. and Needlman, R. (2012) *Dr Spock's Baby and Childcare.* New York: Simon and Schuster

UN General Assembly, *Convention on the Rights of the Child*, 20 November 1989, United Nations, Treaty Series, 1577: 3, available at: www.refworld.org/docid/3ae6b38f0.html [accessed 1st April 2015]

Chapter 3

Role of the adult

by Eleonora Teszenyi

Early childhood experts agree that the first eight years are a very important period of a child's development. This is when significant changes take place setting the foundations for future learning and outcomes (Robinson, 2009; Cowie, 2012; Berk, 2009). Children need to have first-hand experiences with sensitive and responsive adults, together with play opportunities to develop an understanding of themselves and the people and objects around them. Since learning and development are driven by children's desire to make sense of the world, adults may review and consider their role in relation to who children really are (not just what they can do) and what they fundamentally need. Children are social beings and they need love and care as well as support to navigate their way in the complex world of people, wherever they are living and learning. Young children are explorers of the world around them and they need signposting adults; children are thinkers and communicators so they need adults to talk with them and guide their developing thoughts. As the foundation to all of this children are players and they need play partners for their many adventures. Adults are at a distinct biological advantage to fulfil this role: human species are the most neotenous creatures, that is to say that some characteristics of childhood remain in us as adults. Playfulness is in our DNA and we retain some infantile, playful qualities throughout our lifetime (Brown, 2009; Elkind, 2007). There is a general consensus that play is the most effective medium through which children make sense of the world and that children play naturally and spontaneously regardless of their cultural, economic, geographical background (Göncü and Gaskin, 2007). Play offers adults a very firm foundation from which children can truly be seen for who they are.

A child-centred approach acknowledges children as intrinsically curious with a strong exploratory drive, who are active agents in their own learning, particularly when this happens through play. It reinforces a pedagogy that represents itself in practice that is in harmony with children's stage of development at all times. A cross-cultural study in ten different countries concluded that developmentally appropriate practice is what supports young children best (Montie, Ziang and Schweinhart, 2007). This child-centred pedagogy and developmentally appropriate practice together result in a type of 'educare' approach (Rose and Rogers, 2012:6), yet to this integrated approach to care and education, another key element is to be added: nurturing. This is a holistic concept, akin to the 'upbringing' of children, which is the central role of families but which is complemented by schools and settings. It has much in common with the concept of social pedagogy (as used in Germany, Hungary or Denmark) and it can be considered as education in its broadest sense. In international contexts and in multicultural settings that nurturing may be problematic if it is not explained to and explored with parents and carers (and more about parents and carers appears in Chapter 4). There does not exist yet a common language to describe the relationship of effective early years teachers with the children that they work with. One of the ways in which this is being considered is through the notion of intercultural competence, both in children and in their teachers. Cross cultural contact between children and between adults is a strong feature of much international teaching, so intercultural competence offers an approach to communication and cooperation that is attractive. Play looks different in different cultures and environments and early years teachers need to be sensitive to this. This is well described by Brooker (2002) when she describes the small differences in family life - in parenting practices, in perspectives on childhood, and in beliefs about work and play amongst a group of four year old children starting school. She notes how big a difference these make to children settling in and learning confidently at school. She notes the ways in which children are challenged as they adapt to school life during their early days, when playing in the sand is a new experience for example or when role play is based on an unfamiliar environment. The value of effective communication, the respecting of ways of living and ways of being that teachers do not share are crucial to supporting young children well and this can be done through well planned and appropriate play opportunities.

To support children's learning and development, adults fulfil three major roles: a caring, a nurturing and an educating role. These are inseparable, intrinsically connected and bonded together by play. So in effect, the adult is viewed as a playful carer, a playful nurturer and a playful educator all in one. In international contexts the meaning of those roles may not be seen in the same way. Where children are cared for by maids or by nannies they (and their employers) may not see that role as a playful one or natural play responses may be limited by the hierarchy surrounding a maid's role. This is discussed in Chapter 5, about partnership and communication with parents. Where staff in varied international settings are charged with the role of nurturing young children from a range of backgrounds, they may find that their cultural context sees this role very differently to that of the home culture of some or many of the children that they support. This poses a challenge for individual practitioners and for international and multicultural schools and settings. This is addressed in a variety of ways, for example in the case study from Mexico and from Indonesia where children are supported in different ways. The practice described in Chapter 4 highlights the role of the educator in terms that are not reliant on the context nor the curriculum that is offered to young children. What children need to be effective learners is not confined by curricula but is strongly located in the ways in which adults work with them.

A child's learning and development can be viewed from three major perspectives: the empiricist, nativist and interactionist perspectives. In considering the role of the adult across international settings these inform the role of the adult. The three approaches are on a continuum where on one end of the spectrum there is the adult who is an active agent of development and the child is a passive recipient. Play has a very particular nature in such an environment, being adult directed and controlled. In this model learning and development is very much determined by the adult, this is a decreasingly valued approach in the 21st century. The other end of the continuum represents an approach where the child is considered active and the adult is passive and the process of learning and development is driven primarily by the child and their play does not benefit from the challenge and stimulus of a contributing adult. As with the other extreme approach, effective settings across continents follow this practice less and less. Between these two, situated in an area across the middle, is a stance where there is a balance between the child and the adult being active and/or passive in the learning process in a rather intersubjective way. This approach is characterised by reciprocity, sensitivity, responsiveness and constant adjustment to the viewpoint of the other, all of which can be accomplished in a very diverse range of settings. Adults in their engagement with children travel along this continuum according to a number of factors; amongst them are cultural, historical, economical or societal factors. The position that the adults take along this continuum may even be due to community and/or individual values and this is a challenge often addressed in international schools. Often it is influenced by the combination of several sets of values and these can either dovetail or contradict one another. An acute awareness of the adults' own backgrounds along with that of the children's backgrounds will determine the stance they take when engaging with children in their care. The value and ethos of the setting play a key role in establishing the tone for learning amongst the youngest members of the school. Where learning and development are understood and values are shared amongst the team and with parents and carers then children are most likely to learn effectively in the care of appropriate adults.

Caring, according to Noddings (2003: 24), 'involves stepping out of one's own personal frame of reference and into the other's'. Care for young children must be sensitive, personalised and always in response to the child's needs and bids for attention. Cultural values can affect this in the early years setting, where the values of staff from one culture rub up against the values of parents and carers from another, or where a school setting sets its values on the needs of older children and the drive for attainment rather than taking account the developmental and learning needs of the youngest members of the school community. Senior school staff support effective early years provision best when they value and understand the role of the adult in supporting the youngest members of their community. Interestingly it is often the role of the early years teacher to influence and help them to do this. That is one of the reasons why the understanding of child development and a strong personal pedagogy discussed in Chapters 1 and 2 is so important. To bring learning through play to appropriate prominence in an early years setting it must be able to be justified.

The need to defend caring as key to the role of the teacher in the early years is particularly important at a time when young children's lives are more regulated and institutionalised than ever before. England has finally achieved an integrated approach to care and education, which recognises the educational value of care practices in children's development, and much of this practice makes its way into international schools. In England, a successful approach to caring for young children is achieved by key persons (Elfer, Goldshmied and Selleck, 2012), with whom children develop secondary attachments, secure, stable relationships, and from whom they receive concentrated attention and intimate bodily care. In international settings the need for continuity of care must also be recognised to enable children to flourish through the same set of interpersonal and personal skills. Children who move often and who are working in an additional language can participate in play from a very early stage of entry to the setting as long as the opportunities for play are founded on children's interests.

Gerhart (2004) claims that love matters to young children; the first two years of life is the time when the social brain is shaped and foundations for patterns of future emotional experiences with other people are laid. Some children will be in settings at this age so are parents comfortable with practitioners loving their children? Page (2011: 312) argues for 'professional love', which does not compete with parental love; rather, complements it. It has to be acknowledged that the issue of 'love' in professional care in England is a sensitive subject and it requires further examination. It is not so much of a troubled concept across central Europe where warmth and love from the caregiver are prioritised by parents when placing their children in institutional care. Kissing, holding, stroking children are acceptable, in fact desirable, in early years practice to support children's emotional development. Caring adults understand that young children learn to love by experiencing being loved. In Hungarian kindergartens, for example, care, nurturing and education are intrinsically connected. This is reflected in the informal terminology children and parents use for kindergarten pedagogues: 'óvó néni', which translates as 'protective auntie', and the assistant 'dajka', the English equivalent of which is 'nanny'. Regardless of the informal terminology, pedagogues are respected as professionals and the love they give to children is undoubtedly considered as professional love. This notion of professional love is not always widely explored in schools and settings, though it offers the best and most fulfilling experience to young children and to their teachers. Cultural practices, perspectives on 'growing up' and highly attainment oriented parental views can make the notion of professional love undervalued or seen as irrelevant in some contexts. Here the role of the early years teacher must embrace the justification of a pedagogy that meets the needs of children and in which the children interact with effective play partners, their teachers.

Bronfenbrenner's ecological theory (1979) asserts that humans do not develop in isolation but in a complex inter-relationship of four systems: microsystems –the immediate environment of a child, directly influencing development; mesosystems – the interactions between the environments the child directly participates in; exosystems – environments the child does not directly participate in but has an impact on their life or development; and macrosystems – the general organisation of social institutions in the wider society in which the child exists. To understand a child's development holistically, the complex interactions between these different levels of the ecological system must be taken into account. This is particularly important when children face changes and transitions including moving from home to early years care provision, for example, or moving from one nation to another as a more extreme example. Children's ability to adapt to changing environments is primarily supported by their parents (and in some cases those employed by their parents), who provide the most influential context for them to grow up in. This must be in parallel with sensitive caregivers in schools and settings (Desforges and Abouchaar, 2003; Sylva, Melhuish, Sammons, Siraj-Blatchford and Taggart, 2004). For children who are 'third country kids' (mentioned in Chapter 4) then the role of the teacher is more critical. How children are welcomed, how they are brought into the community of the setting and how they are supported is key to the effectiveness of international transitions. Though sometimes challenging, it should be seen as the adults' privilege to be involved with families in the formative years of a child's life. Teachers complement what parents do with/

for their children in a way that adds value: by using their professional skills of nurturing alongside the more readily recognised attributes of their roles. It is important in cross cultural contexts that this is explicit and that parents and schools understand the complexity of settling children and providing them with on-going support and the opportunity to be confident learners.

In a world where 'change is the default setting of our society' (Brooker, 2008:3) it is the adults' responsibility to nurture young children to be able to adjust to this ever-changing world and to develop resilience or as Jarvis (2008: 190) puts it, 'social hardiness for life'. But what skills do children need to stand fast in this future that is so unpredictable? How are these skills developed in a variety of contexts across the globe? Much is connected to personal, social and emotional development – the foundations for dispositions for life-long learning. In any high quality setting staff will be able to support children to know and understand their own feelings, to begin to understand the feelings of others and to form meaningful relationships. Such development is significantly facilitated by play. How this may be done will be arbitrated by the context but must be clearly understood by the teacher and all of the early years team, as well as being a recognised and valued part of the school ethos. As children develop in a secure and caring setting they will learn to take responsibility for their own learning and for their social support as well as gaining greater intrinsic motivation, self-disciple and skills of self-organisation. Claxton (2005) asserts that adults need to help children develop nimble minds - skills of adjustability for the future that is unknown and unimaginable. Early years teachers see daily this nimble mind at work in play and can praise, encourage and value this to support flexibility of thinking and what is called in adults 'thinking outside the box' but for children can be labelled as 'being silly'. This double standard plays to the lack of understanding of play as learning. When considering what Taber (2009: 90) calls 'a simple truth' that education is 'what's left when you've forgotten everything you were taught at school', the role of the adult in helping young children develop life-long learning skills, positive attitudes and dispositions comes into focus: the skills that are not learnt through instruction. Our knowledge of the world is expanding daily and transmitting knowledge is very unlikely to serve children in the future. The primary role of the adult is to enthuse and motivate children; early years teachers need to uncover, as opposed to cover the curriculum at hand, to initiate investigation of subjects and of phenomena that are worthy of children's attention (Katz, 2011). A playful pedagogical approach is most appropriate with young children, since play, indeed, is children's work (Paley, 2005).

A number of studies have confirmed that the role of the adult (teacher, practitioner or pedagogue) is of great significance in children's learning and development, particularly in the early, formative years. Hopkins' (2013) points out that the teacher or pedagogue matters more than the pedagogical model they adopt. Similarly, the findings of Rowe's (2003) international evidence-based research suggest that what matters most to children is the quality of teachers and teaching; in particular, a personalised, child-centred approach where a child receives 'anchored attention' (Roberts, 2010: 73). So as an early years teacher in an international and/or multicultural context, how might the role of the teacher be understood? A knowledge of the curriculum adopted by the setting is taken as read, but is not the over-riding concern in this book. The role of the adult as the leader of playful learning is. Some practical things are worth noting here: the importance of having time for every child in a way which lets them know that they are important to you; having respect for features of their lives that are different to your own and those of other children in the setting; being respectful of their feelings and not being afraid to show them your feelings; reflecting their home experience within the setting through resources and ways of being; being a play partner who though more able in many ways is also able to learn from the child; sharing the learning environment willingly with significant adults in the child's life and most importantly having confidence to show profession love for all of the children that you teach. There are many other things that are bound into the role of a truly effective early years teacher but this crucial role has been well and briefly described by Paley (2013: 48) in this statement:

> I would want teachers who look for opportunities every day to make children happy, and who find ways to make their classrooms fair, equitable, and inclusive. Now that's something that I would treasure and promote.

Paley (1991: xii) reminds us that teaching is a 'moral act'. Early years teachers' ultimate goal is for children to be well-balanced, well-rounded, happy individuals who are able to develop dispositions that serve them well in their lifelong learning.

References

Berk, L. E. (2009) *Child development.*(8th Edn) Boston: Pearson Education, Inc.

Bronfenbrenner, U. (1979) *The ecology of human development.* Cambridge, MA: Harvard University Press

Brooker, L. (2002) *Starting school: Young children learning cultures.* Maidenhead: Open University Press

Brooker, L. (2008) *Supporting transitions in the early years.* Maidenhead: Open University Press

Brown, S. (2009) *Play: How it shapes the brain, opens the imagination and invigorates the soul.* New York: Penguin

Claxton, G. (2005) *Learning to learn: a key goal in the 21st century curriculum. In: Futures, meeting the challenge – a curriculum for the future.* London: QCA

Cowie, H. (2012) *From birth to sixteen. Children's health, social, emotional and linguistic development.* Abingdon: Routlegde

Desforges, C. and Abouchaar, A. (2003) *The impact of parental involvement, parental support and family education on pupil achievement and adjustment.* London: DfES

Elfer, P., Goldshmied, E. and Selleck, D. (2012). *Key persons in the early years.* (2nd Edn) Abingdon: David Fulton

Gerhart, S. (2004) *Why love matters.* London: Routledge

Göncü, A. and Gaskins, S. (2007) (Eds) *Play and development: Evolutionary, sociocultural and functional perspectives.* Mahwan,NJ: Lawrence Erlbaum Associates

Hopkins, D. (2013) *Exploding the myths of school reform.* Maidenhead: Open University Press

Jarvis, P. (2008) Building social hardiness for life: rough and tumble play in the early years of primary school in A. Brock, S. Dodds, P. Jarvis and Y. Olusoga (Eds) *Perspectives on Play: Learning for Life,* 175-93. Harlow: Pearson Longman

Katz, L. G. (2011) Current perspectives on the early childhood curriculum. In: House, R. (ed) (2011) *Too much too soon. Early learning and the erosion of childhood.* Stroud: Hawthorn Press

Montie , J.E., Paley, V.G. (2005) *A child's work. The importance of fantasy play.* London: The University of Chicago Press.

Ziang, X. and Schweinhart, L. J. (2007) (Eds) *The role of pre-school experience in children's development: longitudinal findings from 10 countries.* Ypsilanti, MI: High/Scope Press

Noddings, N. (2003) *Starting at home: caring and social policy.* Berkeley, CA: University of California Press

Page, J. (2011) Do mothers want professional carers to love their babies? *Journal of Early Childhood Research, 9,* (3) 310-323

Paley, V. G. (1991) *The boy who would be a helicopter.* Cambridge: Harvard University Press

Paley, V. G. (2005) *A child's work.* Chicago: University of Chicago Press

Paley, V.G. (2013) Getting back on track: The importance of play and story telling in young children's development. *Early Childhood Education: Successes and Challenges (7)*1, 43-50.

Roberts, R. (2010) *Wellbeing from birth*. London: SAGE

Robinson, M. (2009) *Child development from birth to eight. A journey through the early years*. Maidenhead: McGraw Hill

Rose, J. and Rogers, S. (2012) *The role of the adult in early years settings*. Maidenhead: McGraw Hill

Rowe, K.J. (2003) *The importance of teacher quality as a key determinant of students' experiences and outcomes of schooling*. Discussion paper on behalf of the Interim Committee for a NSW Institute of Teachers, Australia

Sylva, K., Melhuish, E., Sammons, P., Siraj-Blatchford, I. and Taggart, B. (2004) *The effective provision of pre-school education project. Final report*. London: DfES

Taber, K.S. (2009) Learning from experience and teaching by example: Reflecting upon personal learning experience to inform teaching practice. *Journal of Cambridge Studies* 4 (1), 82-92.

Chapter 4

Parents supporting early years and play

by Estelle Tarry

There are many facets to supporting and encouraging learning through play. For educators in international schools and multicultural environments it is critical that parents and carers understand that young children's social, emotional, language, physical and cognitive development happens best by learning through play. The impact and importance of parents and carers contribution to their children's development is not in doubt. They are those most likely to enable young children to be prepared for learning and for the school environment (Goodall, Vorhaus, Carpentieri, Brooks, Akerman, and Harris, 2010: 73).

While focusing on the importance of parental support for learning, this chapter explores world organisations, governments, school and curriculum perspectives on parents/carers involvement and engagement, specifically issues surrounding international schools and multicultural contexts. The role of teachers to engage effectively with parents and carers is also considered. A wide range of issues come into play when developing effective partnership with parents in international contexts; parents' background and educational expectations, internationally mobile families and 'Third culture kids' for example.

Parental involvement is sometimes regarded simply as parents being involved in school trips, parents evenings, social events such as fairs and school performances. However parental engagement can and should be much wider and more active than this. Goodhall *et al.*, (2010: 14) identify parental engagement as being significantly in 5 areas. Learning at home for older children includes help with homework and subject skills in many cases. For young children it encompasses a range of other non-subject skills and the ways in which parents can foster talents, attitudes, values, aspirations and pro-social behaviour. Communication as a part of parental engagement includes communication both to and from the school and family. In-school activities which parents and carers might take part in as volunteers include helping in classrooms, attendance at parents evenings, field trips or being part of the audience for a school performance or presentation. Sometime parental engagement includes being part of school or setting decision making, for example by being a governor or being a member of other committees and advisory groups. Collaboration with the wider community beyond the school is a further form of parental engagement. This might be organisations or family contributions to the school or as a contributor to the community as a member of the school.

Over at least the last couple of decades, across the world, there has been a plethora of research, reports, literature and government policies and acts highlighting parental involvement and engagement; Redding (1997), USA No Child Left Behind (2002), UK Every Child Matters (2004). More recently world organisations and governments have highlighted and supported the involvement and engagement of parents in school and identified specifically that early involvement pays dividend later (Emerson, Fear, Fox and Sanders [Australian Research Alliance for Children and Youth] 2012; Egan [Save the Children UK], 2012; OECD, 2011; DCSF, 2008).

There is UK governmental advice for schools, staff, parents and prospective parents, alongside other information and regulation. There is also guidance for British Schools Overseas (BSO). Much of the guidance, in the UK and elsewhere, concerns provision, attainment and assessment. However for the youngest children there are other issues. These are often implicit rather than overt in both regulations and guidance and so schools and setting that are international and/or multicultural have decisions to make for themselves about how best to engage parents and carers in early education.

The International Baccalaureate School Programme (IB) set standards and guidance for practice, and is used in many international schools and settings. The responsibility of settings using this programme to take appropriate actions within and beyond the school community is explicit and this certainly has implications for the engagement of parents across the age range. For parents of the youngest children this has particular resonance. The Council of International Schools (CIS) like others includes through its accreditation standards the requirement to share information with parents and carers. What this might entail and how it might be done is less explicit across curriculum documentation and so schools and teachers take on the important role of maintaining good parent and carer relationships.

Implicitly or explicitly schools pass on the central cultural values of the particular school depending, among other things, on where the teachers are from. The schools can be limited to a cultural specific pedagogy and therefore it can be 'difficult to engender truly world-minded views of teaching and learning' (Sylvester, 2001: 193). Sylvester goes on to suggest that schools should consider the merit of the curriculum goals rather than the fact that it is based on the country of origin of the curriculum that is being implemented. In this book the curriculum is not under consideration other than as a framework for effective pedagogy and what is best for young learners, that is to say learning through play. How parents view play and its role in learning is important in both international schools and multicultural contexts.

International school parent communities are diverse and can be very different from one international school to another; expatriate parents with either one or both parents working in national or international businesses may be a key parent group. Local elites or affluent (in local terms) nationals may be numerous among the families associated with the school. All families have different reasons for sending their children to an international school. It can be for the curriculum that is offered, the range and quality of educational facilities, teachers' qualifications, extra-curricular activities, English language support, lack of confidence in the national education system, as well as for social and cultural capital such as perceived better social status. Value is also attached to the potential for better qualifications including the access to national universities and (as is clearly seen in the Mexico case study) universities in the UK/USA and Australia and the school's reputational capital. This diversity of reasons and others bring parents and carers to international and multicultural settings with their young children for whom many of these issues are long in the future.

Parents have different educational perspectives too. They may also have different expectations and aspirations for their children in the early years than they do for older ages. Educational expectations may vary from culture to culture, there may be more expectations regarding rigour, more emphasis on reading, writing and arithmetic, some gender and religious expectations, as well as perceptions of the role of the parent within the school. Some parents may have a more holistic approach with regards to the social, emotional and educational development of their young child.

Sometimes the parents' expectations of schooling in the early years may cause conflict with the school expectations, ethos and curriculum. Some families' home cultures are very hierarchical and teachers are considered or perceived to be 'experts' in the education of children. This may well be the case but parents remain the experts in their own children. However a view of teachers as experts can lead to the perception that it is solely the role of the teachers to educate the child. This can result in parents refraining from school participation. Respect for educators has both positive and negative implications. It can lead to disengagement of families with the school and no early years teacher wants that for the children in their care. However it can mean that the pedagogy and practice of the setting is largely not challenged. Again strong early years teachers are keen for the approaches that they use to be understood and to be supported by parents. Getting this to happen takes effort (as described well in the Uganda case study).

In a multicultural environment, as in any other, the school must be aware of the diversity of its community. Sensitivity to parental expectations sometimes comes into conflict with widely held teacher views of effective practice and this must be addressed. For example, some parents are not keen for their children to role play particular activities, such as farm play and associated story-making by the children. A school needs to find ways to both respect and challenge children's right to play with the resources of the setting. This is done in part by ensuring that parents are made aware of the ways in which their young children will be educated in the school, as much as they are aware of the curriculum and qualifications offered to older children. Prospectuses which explain learning through play and why it is important can be helpful as well as enthusiastic explanations by staff during school visits by new families.

International schools may have a high number of internationally mobile families, who move country every few years, and possibly as a consequence the children become 'Global Nomads', where the children may develop a 'third culture' (Langford, 2004) formed from elements of the first 'home' culture and the second 'host' culture. This can be the case for young children as well as for primary and secondary age pupils. What frequent movers need in early education is a secure environment and this is well described in Chapter 5. Effective provision will provide this through high quality staffing and an effective learning environment. Activities that engage young learners should do so for children from different cultures, language groups and family circumstances. Schools and settings need to communicate to parents what they do to provide this and be able to justify it. Supporting staff working with the children and the management teams of schools to do that is one of the primary purposes of this book. Early years teachers often endure the misguided view that they 'just play' all day and so it is important to be able to explain the vital learning that takes place in play (as explained passionately in the Italy case study).

Another area in which parents and schools need clarity of communication is issues encountered when there are maids and nannies in the home. This can have implications for the children and conflict with school expectations can arise. Bradley (2010) carried out a study into the phenomenon of maids in the home environment of young children and the implications for practice in two international schools. She suggests that 'the maid arguably plays a significant role in many families' (p.23) and quite often become the main carer or plays a 'major role in caring for the children of the family' (p.2), having an 'extensive list' of things that they do, such as dressing the children, getting them ready and taking them to school, and, playing and engaging with them (Bradley, 2010: 75). This is likely to put young children into a position of differing values and expectations from their carers and their teachers. Independence skills promoted by early years teachers may not be well understood or even resented by young children who are used to having all of their needs met. Schools can find this a challenging issue to address, with maids feeling that their role is being diminished if the school successfully helps young children to be more independent. Part of this is because school activity may differ vastly from home activity, as Bradley (2010) recalls, resulting in interesting and extreme behaviour,

> 'At the age of three, a particular child only interacted in the kitchen role play area; his family have four maids but his maid was also the family cook. When he was four, he regularly insisted on doing things for others: he carried chairs around the classroom for his peers, dressed them for swimming and insisted on fetching my lunch from my office every day. He appeared to emulate maid behaviour'. (Bradley, 2010: 28)

International schools can alleviate or cater for a situation where children are perceived to display characteristics of over reliance upon maids. The approaches vary from a 'no maids in school' policy to training maids with clear and consistent school expectations of the roles of adults or teachers and teaching assistant modelling behaviour. The sharing of specific rules/responsibility roles in the class with classroom organisation that reflects children's responsibility can help reduce conflicting experience for the child as maids become familiar with the independence skills their charges are expected to show in school. For older children refusal to accept home work done by maids and even the suggestion for families to have governesses not maids at home (Bradley, 2010: 100) have been considered. The issue of maids may be a re-occurring theme but it is not appropriate to categorically state that maids should or should not be involved with the school. International schools may have maids working in them as part of the staff. However maids of the school and home could attend workshops in conjunction with the parents on the supportive role of the maid in their context. Much sensitivity is needed to set up and run such events successfully, they also need to be followed up to help the negotiated good practice to be sustained.

For any parents with children in school, they do need support from and engagement with the school. It is useful, perhaps essential, for the school and individual teachers to implement and promote strategies to support these parents. Good communication may take place via newsletters (perhaps in more than one language) and/or an 'open door policy';

creating a family friendly environment. As mentioned earlier, in some cultures, parents may perceive the school as being the main provider for their child's education and therefore may need more support and encouragement to visit the school and the class. Non-engagement and non-involvement might have nothing to do with being busy or being disinterested in their child's schooling. Therefore international schools may need to provide parental induction programmes and information packs. The sharing of information about how parents can support their children's school and be part of the wider school community is always valuable. Different approaches and strategies need to be implemented to reflect and respect parents' backgrounds, their understanding and knowledge of the school, their awareness of the curriculum and children's learning. Some schools use workshops on parents' role and the school curriculum. Most international schools already provide reports and parents evenings on the children's academic and social and emotional development. This happens once the child is established in the school and some information needs to be shared before this, perhaps through the school prospectus or brochures on learning or during a pre-entry visit. Seeing young children learning through play provides an ideal opportunity for discussion of how children are learning and the pedagogy of the setting.

There is no definitive list of specific strategies that will be effective and supportive for all international schools, for all teachers, for all teaching assistants, for all children or for all parents. There are so many variable factors from one context to another. The case studies included in this book show some of the strategies real schools are using and their effectiveness for them. The case studies bring to life the issues discussed in this and other chapters.

Ultimately all parents and carers can help their young children achieve their full potential by spending time with them, initiating talk and play. Work in partnership with schools and teachers should not be problematic if there is willingness on both sides to listen and to learn. Schools and teachers need to support and enable busy parents to play an active role in their children's development both in and out of school by being creative in the support they offer. The expectations and aspirations of parents, and their involvement and engagement, are likely to be key predictors of their child's later achievement, their dispositions and their attitudes.

References

Bradley, G. (2010) *The 'maid phenomenon ': home/school differences in pedagogy and their implications for children in two international schools in the Middle East,* University of Bath: Unpublished EdD

Department for Children, Schools and Families, (DCSF), (2008) *The impact of parental involvement on children's education,* Annesley; DCSF publications

Egan, D. (2012) *Communities, families and schools together: a route to reducing the impact of poverty on educational achievement in schools across Wales.* Cardiff: Save the Children [online]. Available: www.savethechildren.org.uk/sites/default/files/images/ Communities-families-and-schools-together-report.pdf [20th January 2015]

Emerson, L., Fear. J. Fox, S., and Sanders, E. (2012) *Parental engagement in learning and schooling: lessons from research.* A report by the Australian Research Alliance for Children and Youth (ARACY) for the Family School and Community Partnerships Bureau: Canberra

Goodall J., Vorhaus J., Carpentieri J., Brooks G., Akerman R. and Alma Harris (2010) *Review of best practice in parental engagement,* London: Department for Education

Hayden, M. (2006) *Introduction to international education: International Schools and their communities.* London: Sage Publications

Hayden M. and Thompson J. (2012), *Taking the IPC forward; engaging with the international Primary Curriculum*, (Eds), Woodbridge; John Catt Publication.

Langford, M. (2004) 'Global nomads, third culture kids and international schools', in Hayden, M. and Thompson, J.J. (Eds) *International education; principles and practice,* 28-43. London: Kogan Page

OECD, (2011) What can parents do to help their children succeed in school? *PISA in focus*; no.10

Redding, Sam (1997) *Parents and learning,* International Academy of Education and the International Bureau. Lausanne: PLC

Sylvester, B. (2001) 'Through the lens of diversity: Inclusive and encapsulate school mission' in *International education; principles and practice,* Hayden M. and Thompson J. (Eds) 184-196, London: Kogan Page

Chapter 5

A space to learn: Providing a generous environment

by Gillian Sykes

The phrase 'a generous environment' belongs to the great educational pioneer Susan Isaacs (1885-1948). This best describes what committed early years teachers endeavour to provide for young children through the learning spaces that they occupy with them. The phrase 'learning space' will be used throughout this chapter as the term 'classroom' is one which is often avoided in the early years as it suggests an image of a sterile, institutionalised, perhaps even austere room. This sweeping statement could be seen by many as rather disparaging. Whilst this is not the intention it does raise some questions. This chapter seeks to provoke early years teachers to look at their environments with fresh eyes and from the children's perspective and to consider what a 'generous environment' should look like for particular communities of children. Working in an International School, communities of children will be culturally diverse but the rights of these children will remain the same. Careful, thoughtful planning of the learning space should ensure that children feel a sense of ownership and are able to become confident and resilient learners, to have a sense of belonging and a positive self-identity.

This chapter will provide 'food for thought' and seeks to elicit self-evaluation by teachers of the learning spaces they provide. Views of past and present pioneers will help to challenge the environments of uniformed materials and homogenous schedules and standards. By raising questions this chapter should support examination and justification of the decisions taken to create environments which Curtis and Carter (2003) state enrich rather than diminish human potential.

There are a plethora of innovators, old and new, from whom early years teachers draw knowledge and inspiration. As far back as the 1600s educationalists were developing varied philosophies and it is interesting to ponder what Western education systems would have been like without the influences of Comenius, who for example introduced the notion of obtaining ideas through objects rather than words. Pestalozzi (1746 – 1827), the Swiss social reformer and educator, proposed educational methods which were child centred and promoted physicality to support intellectual development. Interestingly his motto of educating the 'head, hand and heart' is one which has been adopted by and shown in the case study from the Netherlands. Active, child centred learning requires adults to create an environment to support what are now known as the Characteristics of Effective Learning located in the Early Years Foundation Stage (Early Education, 2012).

There are also many contemporary pioneers who have helped to shake the foundations of what had previously been conceived as effective learning environments and which are now viewed as lacking, if not worse. Greenman (1988) keen to see early learning environments transformed, used the term 'places for childhood' to challenge people's thinking. His seminal text 'Caring Places, Learning Spaces' (republished in 2005) has been used widely to design and redesign environments and playgrounds. The very title of his book supports reflection upon the diverse needs of a learning space. A major theme of his writing is based on the premise that time and space are inseparable, and that the time spent in a place influences perceptions of that space. He goes on to say that long periods of time in a confined space can lead to feelings of oppression. This is particularly thought provoking as many children are in settings for long periods of time. It raises the question of how we offer environments which provide for the constancy that builds security as well as variety and stimulation.

The globally respected nurseries of Reggio Emilia, in Northern Italy refer to the environment as the 'third teacher'. Malaguzzi (1987) explained this by asserting that 'there are three teachers of children: adults, other children and their physical environment'. This philosophy further heightens teachers' awareness of the power of an effective environment. He further states 'we value space because of its power to organise ...... and its potential for sparking all kinds of social, affective and cognitive learning' (cited in Fraser and Gestwicki, 2002). This ethos requires teachers to review every nook and cranny of the learning environment and to look at the messages they may convey. It speaks of a flexible space which is responsive to the interests of the children and promotes a sense of enquiry based learning.

Modern day pioneer Elizabeth Jarman has revolutionised many teacher's thinking on how to 'set the scene for learning to take place'. Her website at www.elizabethjarmantraining.co.uk is a veritable tardis of case studies and ideas to rethink the learning environment. She emphasises the need to be able to underpin the changes to the learning environment on high quality research and theory. By making observations of the way the children, and their families, interact with the environment, and then reflecting and making informed decisions on these observations serves to create an environment that is fit for purpose and personalised to the group of children it supports. In an international or multicultural context this includes consideration of, and response to, the communities children come from and the languages and cultural heritage they bring with them.

One of Jarman's key principles is that enacted environment and pedagogy are linked and supportive of each other. What teachers know about how children learn should translate into the layout of the available space and the resources and furnishing chosen. She places an emphasis on: de-cluttering, neutral colour schemes, thoughtful storage, natural light, places for group learning and spaces to be alone, calmness, and space indoors and outdoors. This is illustrated in the Indonesian case study where the educators have used glass/mirrors/light to enhance their learning environments. Jarman puts the development of communication and language at the heart of children's learning. This seems to sit comfortably within an International School context where communication, in its widest sense, is seen as a priority.

This series of questions should help to focus and direct planning 'generous environments'

- How are we using current research to develop our learning spaces?
- How are we planning our learning environments to support the 'Characteristics of Effective Learning'?
- Are our environments inviting and personalised for the interests and needs of our children?
- Are we viewing our environments as 'the third teacher'?

With the adoption of the United Nations Convention on the Rights of the Child (UNCRC) (UN General Assembly, 1989) many countries are now embracing the view that children are not passive objects of care, but have their own rights and that these rights apply to all children. Moving beyond the overarching importance of the convention described in Chapter 1, Article 12 within the convention states that: 'Every child has the right to have a say in all matters affecting them, and to have their views taken seriously'. Additionally considering 'childhood' through a sociological lens, it is clear that children are experts in their own life and hold views and opinions worth listening to. Accepting these beliefs is a step towards attributing real value to the participation of children in shaping and designing their learning spaces.

Clark and Moss (2011) have played a significant role in introducing early years teachers to the merit of using the 'Mosaic Approach' in ascertaining young children's insights into what is important to them in a learning space. The Mosaic Approach uses a variety of methods including child interviewing, photography (by the child), tours, map making and observation to create documentation to use in the design of outdoor and indoor spaces. This method also seeks the views of the parents and practitioners who are also deemed as key players in the development of learning spaces. Clark (2010) highlights the importance of the on-going dialogue between all stakeholders, stressing the value of a democracy in transforming classrooms into 'living spaces' which are attuned to each person's capabilities and needs. In the international context this set of stakeholders may be even wider than in other settings. This necessitates additional care to bring about effective communication with families and carers and effective responses to them that go beyond token celebrations of festivals and stereotypical 'dressing up clothes'. In multicultural settings, international or not, respect and engagement are crucial.

Clark relates her findings to those of Gordon *et al* (2000) who had carried out a similar study with secondary school children. Both studies sought the voice of the child/pupils in gathering their views on the shared environments and the activities associated within them. The study categorised the school into three layers: official school, informal school and physical school. Using this model Clark found that young children disclosed little about the formal school which related to curriculum or controlled spaces, or adults involved in 'teaching'. On the other hand, they provided interesting insights into the informal school for example; personal spaces which linked to their self-identity, family members, friends and practitioners (those not directly teaching), to private spaces (children only areas), social spaces, imaginary spaces and caring spaces. However, the physical school provided the greatest catalyst for dialogues, in which they discussed specific places (toilets, outdoors) and key features (lights, ceilings, floors, colour, beauty). Children who find oral communication with their teachers difficult, for cultural or language reasons for example, may be able to share their perceptions of the learning spaces they occupy through photography.

The following questions may support reflection when planning 'generous environments':

- What does the content of the last section tell us in relation to our own setting?
- Do we consider the rights of the child or are we focussing more on their needs?
- How do we involve the children in planning their learning environment?
- How do we know what is important to the children, parents and families and practitioners?

The challenge for those working in International Schools is how to create an environment where all children feel included and feel a sense of belonging. This should be an environment where positive identities can be developed and new identities acquired. Vandenbroeck (2008) states that children are able to constantly 'code switch', and that they adapt their behaviours to different settings and relationships. However the transition into an early years setting is often their first encounter with values and norms which are different to home. With this in mind the learning space provided needs to be an environment which respects the children's multiple identities and celebrates this.

Providing a dynamic, yet constant environment which takes into account diversity and social inclusion is no easy task. Yet remembering a few easy pointers helps to create a mindset through which teachers can begin to provide a space which helps shape identity and reflects values.

Curtis and Carter (2008:12) provide an assessment tool which requires teachers to put themselves in the shoes of a three to six year old and to look at the environment from their perspective. The statements originate from research looking at favourite childhood memories. Teachers should use the statements and a floor plan of the learning space, then number the area where the statement can be seen to be true. Can all of the suggested components be found?

1.	I can see who I am and what I like to do at school and at home
2.	There are comfortable places for my family to sit and talk with me or my teachers
3.	The natural world can be found here (such as objects from nature, animals, and living specimens).
4.	There is something sparkly, shadowy, or wondrous and magical here.
5.	My teacher leaves a special object out each day so I can keep trying to figure out more about its properties and how it works.
6.	There are materials here that I can use to make representations from what I understand or imagine.
7.	I can be powerful and be physically active here.
8.	I can learn to see things from different perspectives here, literally and through assuming roles in dramatic play.
9.	I see my name written, or I get to regularly write my name here.
10.	I get to know my teacher here – what they like, how they spend their time away from school, and which people and things are special to them.

Curtis and Carter go on to say that the following are the elements which should be considered when planning an early years space:

- Connections and a sense of belonging – through maintaining connections with home, providing a welcoming homely environment and helping children to make new relationships within a new context

- Flexible space and open ended materials – to provide a variety of ways for children and adults to use space and materials to pursue their own interests and to learn with and from others
- Natural materials which engage the senses – to fill the environment with aspects of the natural world to stimulate and soothe the senses and sensibilities
- Wonder, curiosity and intellectual engagement – to keep the brain pathways and connections growing and expanding by providing intriguing provocations to discover and explore
- Symbolic representations, literacy and the visual arts – to provide an array of opportunities for multiple intelligences (Gardner, 1983) and the 'hundred languages of children' (Malaguzzi, 1987).

They believe that consideration of these aspects will help shape a positive identity, lasting memories and effective learning experiences for all children. A multicultural setting is likely to embody a wondrous range of experiences. But what does this mean in practice? Every child is unique and has their individual differences. Rather than viewing this as a deficit these differences should be celebrated and relished as a feature of the diversity of the school or setting. Whilst one child enjoys quiet another is constantly on the go. In the same way one child may like building and constructing whilst another likes to take on a variety of roles. The role of the teacher is to get to know each child and provide areas and materials which connect with their preferences, interests and needs.

There are some final points for consideration when developing early childhood spaces. Young children need to move and it is known that the body and brain develop together in the young. As the brain develops sequentially, from lowest physical areas to the higher thinking areas, then children need to move to support this neurological process. Therefore as a teacher providing an uncluttered space for children to move both indoors and outdoors meets that need, whatever the child's background or current level of competence as a learner. Children are naturally curious and this curiosity needs nurturing and feeding. Albert Einstein stated 'I am neither very clever nor especially gifted. I am only very, very curious'. With this in mind early years teachers should universally be providing a rich environment to fuel enquiring minds. What this might look like is less certain, as it must reflect the community of the setting in its widest sense.

It is well recognised that imagination and creativity are central to learning and that experiences which allow for creativity and imagination will fuel the brain and develop thinking, knowing and making choices. Provision needs to therefore accommodate our young scientists, designers, novelists, and mathematicians. Alongside this children need concrete experiences to explore and experiment. Such play is the vehicle by which children learn to persevere, attend to detail, concentrate and learn the rules of social behaviour. Therefore environments which provide continuous provision to enable these opportunities, and the selection of that provision must also meet the needs of the community. That means that change and development will be ongoing as children enter and leave the setting. For many schools and setting this movement is an annual process but in international schools the group may change in size and character throughout the year. That means that the environment will be continually responding to these changes. These are not monumental changes but additions and enhancements which help children to feel valued, recognised and welcome.

In drawing this chapter to a conclusion it must reflect back to where it started and ask again the question what is meant by a 'generous environment'. This chapter set out to deliberately challenge existing learning environments and to help early years teachers to consider if the learning space offered is accommodating the needs of a particular, complex group of children.

Community Playthings (2014) have a super free resource entitled 'The Irresistible Classroom'. The introduction of this resource states that the child does the learning, the teacher facilitates the learning and the environment must support them both. This puts a great importance onto the learning space.

Deliberate and ponder the learning space from the child's point of view:

If this is not a place where tears are understood, where do I go to cry? If this is not a place where my spirits can take wing, where do I go to fly? If this is not a place where my questions can be answered, where do I go to seek? If this is not a place where my feelings can be heard, where do I go to speak? If this is not a place where you'll accept me as I am, where can I go to be? If this is not a place where I can try to and learn to grow, where can I just be me?

William J. Crockett.

References

Clark, A. (2010) *Transforming children's spaces. Oxon:* Routledge

Clark and Moss (2011) Listening to young children: *The Mosaic Approach. (*2nd Ed.) London: NCB

Community Playthings (2014) *The irresistible classroom.* East Sussex: Community Playthings

Curtis, D. and Carter, M. (2003) *Designs for living and learning: Transforming early childhood environments.* St Paul, MN: Redleaf Press

Early Education (2012) *Development Matters in the Early Years Foundation Stage (EYFS).* London: Early Education

Fraser, S. and Gestwicki, C. (2002) *Authentic childhood: Exploring Reggio Emilia in the classroom.* Albany, N.Y.: Delmar

Gardner, H. (1983) *Frames of mind: The theory of multiple intelligences.* New York: Basic Books.

Gordon, T., Holland, J. and Lahelma, E. (2000) *Making spaces: Citizenship and difference in schools.* London: Macmillan Press

Greenman, J. (1988) *Caring places, learning spaces.* Redmond, Washington State: Exchange Press

Jarman, E. (2009) *The communication friendly spaces approach.* Kent: Elizabeth Jarman Ltd

Malaguzzi, L. (1987) *The hundred languages of children: narrative of the possible.* Reggio Emilia, Italy: Department of Education

Vandenbroeck, M. (2008) cited in Brooker, L. and Woodhead, M. (Eds.) (2008) *Developing positive identities: Diversity and young children.* Milton Keynes: Open University Press

UN General Assembly, *Convention on the Rights of the Child, 20 November 1989, United Nations, Treaty Series,* 1557: 3, available at: http://www.refworld.org/docid/3ae6b38f0. html [Accessed 1st April 2015]

Chapter 6

Learning outdoors: Come rain or shine

by Gillian Sykes

Having considered the learning environment indoors, then it is now important to give consideration to the outdoor spaces in which young children learn. It is now widely recognised that the outdoor space is just as important to young children's learning as the indoor space, and for some it is regarded as more valuable. Reflecting on the question 'What is my earliest play memory and where was I?' results in a large percentage of adults recounting experiences of being in the outdoors. Memories of poking around in mud, hunting for bugs, building dens and splashing in puddles are close to the heart of many adults. Watching young children and their families in a park or on a beach reveals that for many the outdoors is a more natural and fulfilling environment.

There is now a wealth of literature which praises the unique qualities of the outdoors for the benefits it can provide for young children's learning and development. Indeed countries such as the Scandinavian nations, Germany, the USA and the UK have rich histories of outdoor education. This chapter will investigate the spread of outdoor learning, and in particular, it will look at its impact on learning. Additionally this chapter will seek to briefly address the challenges and barriers to accessing the outdoors in some of the contexts and climates experienced in international school communities.

Across the ages there has been considerable interest in the value of the outdoors to young children's learning. Unlike the changing landscape of opinion on the indoor environment, early years pioneers have generally agreed that the outdoors is beneficial to young children's learning. Once again the names of Rousseau and Pestalozzi, Froebel and Steiner are relevant and their influence in shaping the use of the outdoors in early years education across Europe is well established. Froebel for his 'gardens for children', now known as Kindergartens, and Steiner with the value he placed on nature and the changing seasons. In the UK, Margaret McMillan and her sister Rachel are celebrated for recognising the benefits the outdoors had on improving the health and well-being of children in the early 1900s. Margaret McMillan's famous quote: "The best classroom and the widest cupboard is roofed only by the sky" sums up how many early years practitioners now view the outdoors. The McMillan sisters established the first Open Air Nursery in Deptford, London in 1914. This carefully planned children's garden was not 'thrown together', it was thoughtfully organised with the children's interests and needs central to its design (Bilton, 2010). Bilton also notes the relevance of this work to contemporary practice. The creation of a planned space helps children to foster a love of nature, promotes healthy physical activity and social inclusion. The real life environment avoids a task-structured environment and offers ever-changing first-hand sensory experiences. A deliberate, considered place where children and adults can play and learn together.

However the strength of these attitudes have flowed and ebbed, but the opinion in Northern Europe has been consistent and has resulted in it becoming a 'cultural norm' to provide high quality outdoor provision (Knight, 2012 cited in Papatheodorou and Moyles). The impact of this on the development of the children in these countries has been significant. Therefore many countries have adopted this well respected practice and have recognised that the outdoors should be accessed no matter what the weather. The Norwegian age-old saying 'there is no such thing as bad weather, only wrong clothing' has meant that many early years' schools and settings have invested in wellingtons and waterproofs, sunhats and areas of shade to help their children benefit and learn from the outdoors in all weather conditions.

The well-respected Forest School movement, which began in Scandinavia in the 1950s, is now popular in many countries and provides environments for wilder play and the opportunities for children to connect with nature and learn about sustainability. In Scandinavia, well-established cultural links with nature have meant that it is customary for young children to often spend more time outdoors than they do indoors. However Knight (cited in Papatheodorou and Moyles, 2012:33) reports concerns that modern living, especially technology, is 'eroding this long standing tradition' and that there is now a conscious effort by early years' practitioners in Denmark, Sweden and Norway to continue this effective relationship with the outdoors.

Around the world educators and policy makers are becoming increasingly concerned for the planet and for the health and well-being of those little citizens who will in the future become the new educators and policy makers. Therefore the need to educate young children in recognising the importance of looking after their communities and the planet is becoming internationally accepted. Sara Knight's book *'International Perspectives on Forest School: Natural Spaces to Play and Learn'* provides inspiring case studies from, for example, Brazil, India, South Africa and Slovenia. Her book is especially pertinent for those working in extreme climates or facing the concerns of, for example, potentially dangerous creatures. It must be remembered that unless children are faced with risks how will they understand the nature of risk or learn how to deal with risks. Instead of being risk-averse Gill (2009:76) suggests 'children friendly communities' and that teachers 'reject what might be called the philosophy of protection and instead adopt a philosophy of resilience'. There are now 'risk benefit assessment tools' which can be found and downloaded from Gill's thought provoking web site http://rethinkingchildhood.com. This website also provides ideas for justifying to over anxious parents the advantages of accessing the outdoors. This is likely to be useful in international school settings and multicultural environments in which parents may 'fear' the outdoors or are unaware of its benefits for young learners.

Looking through the case studies and photographs within this book it is clear that many international Schools have already embraced the outdoors as a vital learning area. The photographs provide examples of how to overcome many of the potential obstacles to using the outdoors to facilitate children's learning. Several images show sweeping canopies which help children escape from the direct sunlight and insect repelling plants are described in the Indonesian case study. These challenges to creating usable outdoor learning spaces vary considerably from one context to another. Climate is clearly a first order issue closely followed by local insects and wildlife and potential for disease. It is not surprising that the difficulties of providing high quality outdoor learning experiences overwhelm staff. Having a good experience despite the challenges can change the perception of outdoor learning and so induction of new staff should feature accessing the outdoor learning environment. Established staff that are reluctant can be paired with enthusiasts and often observing the quality of children's learning outdoors is enough to change hearts and minds.

Clearly individual countries have different approaches to childcare and education. This is sometimes to do with the statutory school starting age and sometimes to do with cultural differences. For many less industrialised countries, children often spend a preponderance of their leisure time outdoors; whilst in those countries who are the global drivers of commerce children often have a greater relationship with technology. Yet the increase in research based knowledge and understanding that outdoor play is valuable to young children's development is sweeping the world. In 2005 American writer Richard Louv, wrote his now acclaimed book 'The Last Child in the Woods', and introduced the term 'nature deficit disorder'. In short, the book highlights the effects of 'nature deficit' on the current generation of children and adults in terms of obesity, depression and attention disorders. By signing up to the Children and Nature Network http://www.childrenandnature.org it is possible to be kept up to date with worldwide innovations and research linked to the crucial relationship of nature to young children's development. Findings have shown how access to nature can reduce the stress hormone cortisol, increase the immune defence system and increases cerebral blood flow. Interestingly, Japan (a key global driver) has heeded the concerns of a disconnection with the outdoors and have introduced the practice of shinrin-yoku, or forest bathing. This is a practice now observed by about a quarter of the country.

In England, prior to the introduction of the Foundation Stage (3-5) in 2000 there was little prominence given to the outdoors. Although there was always an understanding of the benefits of the outdoors, there was little encouragement from the government or regulatory bodies to promote or control its use. Often the outdoors was used primarily as a 'playtime' for children to 'let off steam', a notion mentioned in Chapter 2. However, with the introduction of the Foundation Stage and the emphasis it placed on play and independence, practitioners began to develop and use the outdoors to support children's learning. The Early Years Foundation Stage (2008) was greeted, by many, with enthusiasm as it stated as a requirement that quality outdoor experiences should be provided on a daily basis. Alongside this the Labour government published the 'Learning Outside the Classroom Manifesto' (DfES, 2006). This manifesto is once again gaining momentum as 'character education' rises up the government agenda. As educationalists talk about the key character traits that are pre-requisites for academic success, it is hardly surprising that the Council for Learning Outside the Classroom (CLOtC, 2015) are promoting the outdoors. They talk of 'robust evidence about the benefits of learning outside the classroom in helping pupils develop resilience, self-confidence, communication skills and the skills of inquiry and problem solving' (Issue 19, March 2015).

What then are the benefits and advantages of the outdoors to young children and their learning and development? The National Trust Publication 'Natural Childhood' (Moss, 2012) outlines these benefits and advantages in four categories: health, education, communities and the environment. The health benefits are both physical and mental. Childhood obesity continues to be a problem in 'digitally enhanced' western society. When children play outside they are generally more active for longer periods of time and this can benefit their health. Enjoyment of the outdoors as a child lays the foundations for the habits of adulthood. It is commonly agreed that physical activity supports mental well-being. Exposure to nature also reduces stress and aggressive behaviour. One study reported that children suffering from Attention Deficit Hyperactivity Disorder (ADHD) were observed as being three times calmer when they spent time outdoors. Moreover, a recent survey by the National Trust reported that 80% of the happiest people in the UK spent times outdoor.

Sigman (2007) found that exposure to nature meant that children were more able to concentrate, had better self-discipline, achieved more highly in academic studies and had improved awareness and behaviour. They understood more, felt better, and were able to work more cooperatively and were physically healthier. These are hard benefits to ignore and it is not surprising that international schools work hard to provide outdoor learning.

In relation to the benefits of the community, Whyte (2007) writes of the importance of personal geographies and relationships with the local environment to help young children develop a sense of citizenship, belonging and wonder. Children need to have a sense and understanding of their world to enable them to make connections with the wider world. Visits to the local community give children opportunities to observe and ask questions regarding the environment and to develop positive and negative attitudes of the things they like and dislike. This also gives early years teachers the opportunity to challenge some of the preconceived ideas some children may have. This is especially important for many of the children in international schools whose first home may not be within the community where they are educated. By visiting and interacting with the local environment of their school they can begin to develop these important, transferable skills, and to understand the need to respect and value diverse communities.

The final category identified by Moss (2012) is the environmental benefits that come with children accessing the outdoors. David Attenborough said *'No one will protect what they do not care about; and no one will care about what they have never experienced'.* This simple, yet profound statement clearly asserts that unless children know about and experience natural history then they will have no regard for safeguarding it for the future. This is again an area of challenge in international settings. In an geographical area where snakes are dangerous it can be hard to encourage children to include them in their natural love of nature. Early years teachers can help this by teaching children about habitat, and right and wrong places for themselves and for other living creatures. In this way children are not encouraged to show a potential dangerous curiosity of living things they come across in their own locality.

So, it is agreed that there are untold benefits for children accessing the outdoors. What then should outdoor environments look like and what experiences can/should they offer? The assumption by some 'that knowledge acquired indoors is superior to that gained outside' (Bruce, 1987:55 cited in Bilton, 2010:36) must be swept away. To do this planning for use of the outdoors should be done on a daily basis and that the topic of the outdoors is discussed at staff meetings and at induction meetings with parents and families. The outdoors should feature in training and should not be viewed as something that is only applicable to the early years, as is seen in the United Kingdom case study. From the outset the outdoors needs to be recognised as equally valuable to the indoors to encourage a change in mindset.

Established outdoor environments vary greatly and reflect the context in which particular groups of young children play, learn and develop. There will be a range of influencing factors: space available, climatic considerations, availability of natural materials, risk benefit assessments, children's views and ideas, budgets and so the list could go on. A key consideration must be the importance of space to enable children to move. Physical development is probably the most important aspect of child development as it is movement that helps the brain to develop. The body should be acknowledged as a source of information for the young child as everything is learned through the body and its seven sensory systems. The outdoors provides the perfect environment to develop these systems of: balance, proprioception, touch, vision, hearing, taste and smell and to support neurological organisation. Lack of space constrains learning, and this is especially true for young boys. The smallest outdoor space can seem much larger than a small indoor space as the sky is its ceiling. However when the indoors and outdoors are used in conjunction they become a reasonably sized space (Bilton, 2010). Therefore direct access to the outdoors through large sliding doors is preferable, as described in the Indonesian case study. Other desired aspects of the outdoor space are:

- A transitional, partially covered area between the indoors and the outdoors which provides both shade and shelter
- An outdoor area which has direct vision from the indoors
- An area for continuous provision
- An area to 'let off steam'
- A wilder area to connect and learn from nature
- Different surfaces, levels and slopes
- Seating

- Areas for growing
- Storage areas
- Shrubs and trees local to the area
- If at all possible a water supply

It is wise to avoid lots of fixed equipment that is expensive, often needs supervision by staff and is limiting in learning potential. Also avoid plastic and bright colours and instead go for attractive natural features. Taking on board the benefits of nature to young children's development means teacher and other practitioners should ensure that outdoor environments are developed using natural materials, local to the area, and that change and mature with time. The outdoor space, Bilton reminds us, needs to be an attractive, stimulating place for learning, full of endless possibilities. Because of this we should be planning spaces which are flexible and responsive. Many of the case studies have demonstrated their use of the outdoors, all are unique to their school context. As discussed in Chapter 5 the views of children should also be elicited as well as those of their parents and early years teachers. This is no less the case for the design of the outdoor space than any other area of provision. In redesigning an outdoor area the Mosaic Approach (Clark and Moss, 2005) can be used to gather the children's perspectives. Their book 'Spaces to Play' describes a pilot project and provides inspiration for the development of outdoor spaces.

Finally, it is important to consider how these important messages are conveyed to children's parents and families and to the governing bodies of schools. If, as has been fully discussed here, the outdoors is critical for early childhood pedagogy and policy in the 21st century, then involving parents and families in sharing this knowledge and understanding is significant. Parents want what is best for their children and for their future. When parents believe in and trust the schools and those who care and educate their children, they too will begin to value the outdoors more and will be committed to supporting their children's access to the outdoors.

References

Bilton, H. (2010) *Outdoor learning in the early years: Management and innovation.* (3rd Ed) Oxon: Routledge

Clark, A. and Moss, P. (2005) *Spaces to play: More listening to young children using the mosaic approach*. London: NCB

Council for Learning Outside the Classroom (2015) *Members newsletter*. Issue 19, March 2015

Department for Education and Skills (DfES) (2006) *Learning outside the classroom manifesto*. Nottingham: DfES

Gill, T. (2009) *No fear: Growing up in a risk averse society*. London: Calouste Gulbenkian Foundation

Knight, S. (2013) *International perspectives on forest school: Natural spaces to play and learn*. London: Sage

Louv, R. (2005) *Last child in the woods: saving our children from nature-deficit disorder*. Chapel Hill, NC : Algonquin Books of Chapel Hill

Moss, S. (2012) *Natural childhood*. outdoor.nation@nationaltrust.org.uk [Accessed 20th March 2015]

Papatheodorou, T. and Moyles, J. (Eds) (2012) *Cross-cultural perspectives on early childhood*. London: Sage

Sigman, A. (2007) *Agricultrual literacy: Giving concrete children food for thought*. www.face-online.org.uk/resources/news/Agricultural%20Literacy.pdf [Accessed 3rd April 2015]

Whyte, T. (2007) *Personal geographies – children and their local environment* In Austin, R. (Ed) (2007) *Letting the outside in: developing teaching and learning beyond the early years classroom*. Stoke on Trent: Trentham Books Ltd

Indonesia - a shady space for the hot days

Italy - collaboration and cooperation during play

Mexico - Birthday parties, one of the few places children play with each other outside of school

Mexico - The maid becomes the playmate in many situations

Netherlands - Children in freeflow

Netherlands - Freeflow play inside and out

United Kingdom - the joy of mud and sticks

Qatar - Children involved in free play at the start of the Multi-skills unit

Romania - Negotiating building outside

Romania - Sensitive support from an adult

Uganda - Hands on experiences

Uganda - Ship Ahoy

United Kingdom - made structure supported in a natural structure

United Kingdom - older children also enjoying the outdoor learning

Chapter 7

Case Studies

This chapter is composed of case studies from a range of international and multicultural settings, in the words of the people who work in them. The case studies open a window on practice across a broad spectrum of geographical locations, class sizes, physical environments and they are fascinating! These are the words of teachers themselves, their names and school locations appear form part of each case study. The authors of this book thanks all the case study contributors for their generosity in sharing their practice, thanks also go to the schools and the young learners in those schools.

The images in the colour section directly before this chapter have also been provided by our generous school colleagues. The titles of the pictures include the country they come from, so that they can be linked to the case studies in this chapter.

Netherlands: 'What have you done at school today?' - Play as learning

Italy: The importance of play for learning in the early years and beyond

Uganda: When play is a foreign language: transformation of the early years learning environment

Uganda: All change! The transformation of early years learning

Qatar: Making sure learning happens in foundation stage physical education

Romania: 'Is this really teaching?' - The role of the adult in supporting learning

Mexico: The view from here: comments on parents perspectives for joining the early years centre

Indonesia: Not stuck indoors: challenges to outdoor provision in a tropical climate

United Kingdom: Outdoor learning: back to nature

'What have you done at school today?' - Play as learning

Karren van Zoest, Deputy Headteacher, Junior School Leidschenveen, The British School, Netherlands

With over 2200 students aged 3 -18 the British School in the Netherlands (BSN) is a large British school spread across 4 sites in and around the Hague. With three Junior schools and a Senior school, the BSN is able to create a "Family of schools" approach where each individual school has its own personality and sense of identity, but all work together under the umbrella of a common vision, aims and sharing of good practice.

Our belief as a school is that we are "Internationally British". This reflects the changing context of the BSN during the last ten years, with a decline of British students, but a steady increase of international students. This is due to economic changes reflected by major international companies based in the Netherlands. The BSN now has just 26% British students and over 80 other nationalities. Despite this growing trend, research by our marketing department shows that the BSN is a preferred choice of international parents because of its British values and ethos. So whilst the demographic is changing, the school has ensured that those values and beliefs that we hold dear are a strong feature of our schools and carefully balanced with regard to the shift towards a higher level of cultural diversity.

The BSN uses the National Curriculum of England and Early Years Foundation Stage (EYFS) as the core curriculum throughout the 3-18 age range. The emphasis is on creating a learning environment which encourages the growth and development of the whole child. *"Head, Hand and Heart"* where, as well as academic success, practical skills are encouraged, talents are celebrated and emotional growth is nurtured.

In practice this means that learning is not just about what you know, but more importantly it is about reflecting on how you learn, and understanding who you are as a person, both in your learning and in the community. It is about what makes you unique, being proud of that, but always within a culture that promotes motivation to learn and improve.

"What have you done at school today?" is a question asked by parents in over 30 different home languages, at the end of the school day. It is a wonderful experience to hear children talking in their mother tongue about what they have done, but it is a challenge too. In the early years classrooms the number of children speaking English as a first language is very small, approximately 15%. Fortunately we have an amazing common language to communicate through; the language of *play*. I think that children in the EYFS (aged three-five) could teach our world leaders a thing or two about learning to negotiate across different cultures, about communicating their feelings without misunderstandings, and about sharing resources, even if their ideas and goals are different from each other!

At the BSN we recognise the truly astounding power of play in the development of the whole child. How do we do this? Imagine we are standing in a Foundation One classroom, where children are three or four years old. An adult, perhaps the teacher but just as often a teaching assistant (TA), is sitting beside the door on a low chair at the children's eye-level, warmly welcoming each of them individually as their school day begins. A variety of activities, which have been carefully selected to excite and encourage a child's imagination and intellectual curiosity, have been set up and arranged in different parts of the available space. Normally they would be part of a chosen theme *eg* 'People who help us' or 'Animals'. Often resources are linked together to encourage this; cars are placed close to a set of bricks that could become ramps or garages, Lego is in the sand tray which could become an earthquake over flowing a house they have built, or mixing cement to be a builder. There is no right or wrong way to experiment. Play is intentional, planned and most importantly valued, and yet for the children it is a spontaneous, open ended experience, allowing each child to focus and spend time on their own personal development.

The philosophy of using *"Head, Hand and Heart"* to promote our school values is no better exemplified than through play. There is no need to mull over how to pitch an activity at the 'right' level or to spend time 'thinking up' a strategy to motivate children to learn. We observe and reflect on their choices and make note of the learning that is going on. A trained professional is specifically focussed on developing the play around them. The adult skill is in intervening enough to encourage further thinking, developing the child's ideas and supporting their learning, but also knowing when to hold back and let the children lead the play. There is a subtle difference between extending children's play and directing it.

Back in the classroom, a group of children are sitting on the carpet. Two of the three are non- English speakers. Harry is very shy and misses mum, Alice is a confident English speaker who likes to play 'teacher', and the third is a little boy, Sebastian, whose fine motor control is just developing in comparison to his peers. There is a "small world farm", which has been set out with fences and stables. There are also some plain-coloured sorting 'spots' and numbers, scattered nearby. The carpet is close to a role play corner, where a kitchen has been set up. To the untrained eye they appear to be "just playing" but in this one scenario the learning that takes place is amazingly complex.

Harry, gripping tightly onto two of the animals, is sitting watching the two other children. He is insecure and appears to be unable to allow himself to enjoy the farm in front of him. As time goes on he becomes preoccupied by the game that Alice is playing; putting sheep into the barn and then lining them up. She does it over and over again. He leans forward. Alice points at him and says "Come on, line them up!" She points again at his hand and then at the line. Whilst firmly pulling an animal out of his hand, she makes the animal sound and smiles at Harry. Harry caught in the moment joins the game- learning to trust his surroundings and have the confidence to try.

Meanwhile Sebastian takes a handful of animals and walks into the role play kitchen. He puts them onto the table and collects a plate, a small spoon and some dried peas that are standing on the cooker. Using all of his concentration he carefully balances each pea on the spoon and feeds the animals. "Are you finished? Eat it up!" he says, copying the phrases he has heard the teaching staff use at snack time. Sebastian is- *learning to use the language he has heard after only just four weeks at school, and is practising and perfecting his fine motor control at the same time.*

Alice has moved on in her game and has left Harry to continue lining up the animals. She grabs some of the numbers and puts them in order on one of the sorting 'spots'. A teaching assistant (TA) approaches and asks what she is going to do next with the numbers. Alice looks thoughtful but has no answer, so the TA prompts, "You could see if you've got enough numbers for all the animals to have one". Alice immediately jumps up and says "Yes … and I could give them all one and see which is more… and I could find more numbers if I need them!" Alice is- *learning about "More" and "Less" and consolidating her skills of 1:1 correspondence.*

At the BSN our belief in how play supports the schools core values, is reflected in the importance we place on it every day. Play is a highly effective learning medium at our school because the opportunities to be engaged in it are intentional and purposeful. The school environment is a safe, nurturing but also a challenging one, for each and every child. Our children are motivated to learn because it has been a choice; something they want to do and therefore the learning experience is so much more powerful. Play is embraced in all areas. It is an integral part of the life of the classroom; from the teacher planning, the classroom environment, the resources and the bespoke 'green' playgrounds, to the selection and recruitment of staff who understand how to enhance learning through play. Even school timetables and assessment procedures, in fact all of the business of school, reflects our commitment to ensuring quality learning experiences through play, for the children we teach.

Moving on to the future; we aim to further enhance the power of play in children's learning by looking at several areas. Firstly, born into this fast moving technological age, we see an increasing need to model play in our classrooms, with children who are simply more comfortable with a smart screen device, than hands on games and toys. Secondly looking at the balance between school routines, timetables and opportunities for extended play, where a child's ideas can be developed over time, and the moments of disruption to the learning process are kept to a minimum. Finally that outdoor play experiences encourage a greater element of risk and challenge, where experimenting and making connections with the world are as natural as the resources around them; something that many children have had precious little experience of in our safety conscious world. As the world changes around our children perhaps we should remember what Ignacio Estrada (1696 – 1760) said…

"If children can't learn the way we teach, we should teach them the way they learn"

Karren van Zoes

Karren has been Deputy Headteacher of Junior School Leidschenveen, (part of the British School in the Netherlands, BSN for the last five years. Before this she was the Leader of the BSN Foundation Stage Unit. and has a particular interest in the value of play in Early Years provision. Karren is passionate about the role of teaching assistants in the classroom, ensuring that they are well trained and informed, and are therefore a highly effective and integral part of the learning process.

The importance of play for learning in the early years and beyond

Chris Williams, Headteacher of St George's La Storta Junior School, Rome, Italy

St George's British International School is based in Rome and caters for students from 3 to 18 years of age, which means that, as its Junior School located on the main site, we have the advantage of an international setting and being in close proximity to the Senior School. The first enables us to 'borrow' from best practice in the UK and abroad, while the second ensures excellent access to the resources and subject specialisms of the Senior School. As Head, I have endeavoured to make sure opportunities for 'play' both indoors and outdoors, is developed alongside other areas of the curriculum. I firmly believe in the value that play situations create for the social construction of knowledge through talk and the opportunities they provide for 'hard-wiring' of skills taught during focussed teaching time. To this end, all our Early Years Foundation Stage and Key Stage 1 classrooms face onto the playground and have their own protected and well-furnished outside areas for play-based activities.

Our curriculum shadows the National Curriculum of England, taking the best from it, whilst also enriching its content and approach. We have gradually moved from delivering a content driven to a skills-based curriculum, using the Early Years Foundation Stage (EYFS) Learning Goals and the National Curriculum Levels to provide pathways to track developmental and skills progression in all curriculum areas.

We are fortunate to be working closely with Pie Corbett to embed his innovative approach 'Talk for Writing' in Literacy learning at our school. Over the last two years we have found that Talk for Writing works well within an international setting, where many children are English as Additional Language (EAL) learners, because it approaches literacy from a speaking and listening perspective. This complements our focus on play, because it means we can also use structured play activities to provide our children with resources and stimuli to embed their literacy learning. All of this ensures that there are plenty of opportunities for the children to 'speak it' both before and after they 'read it' or 'write it'. A delightful example of this is a reception child's declaration that he was 'rolling the dough' during his outside structured play activity in the cinnamon scented jelly bath, (see the Outdoor Planning Sheet below). It was a perfect link to their Talk for Writing story, 'The Gingerbread Man'. Likewise, in Numeracy, we also place great emphasis on resources that offer concrete approaches to learning such as Numicon, which is effectively used to support numeracy learning in the early years and Key Stage 1, and lends itself well to play activities for those groups working independently during focussed teaching time.

The physical layout of our Junior school with the Foundation and Key Stage 1 classes facing onto the playground and having their own outdoor areas is no accident and it might be useful to explain my rationale for establishing this set up. As a new Head, I knew I had a great deal to learn about the Foundation Stage, since my teaching experience was in Key Stages 1 and 2. The more I learnt, the more I understood how effective the teaching and learning in the Foundation Stage needed to be to ensure that the inner talents and abilities of every child were nurtured and allowed to grow. I began to question the kind of transition we had in place from reception to Year 1 and soon realised that the change in learning experiences from a play-based, learner-centred curriculum in the Foundation Stage, to a more prescriptive teacher-centred experience in Key Stage 1 was too abrupt for many of the children. There needed to be a more gentle transition at this stage in children's learning which incorporated a 'bottom-up' rather than a 'top-down' approach. I also became aware of just how important play is for learning, and realised the need to create opportunities for play within lessons, not only in Year 1, but also Year 2, and beyond. I was guided and supported in reaching this understanding, not only through valuable inset sessions led by experienced practitioners visiting the school, but also by the enthusiasm and conviction of the early years staff I had, and continue to have, the pleasure to work with.

How does this work in practice? How are we able to satisfy the demands of the curriculum and the expectations of our parents by incorporating more opportunities for play within the school day?

First, we work closely with our parents to inform them of the methods we use for teaching and learning at school across the curriculum through regular meetings conducted during the school year. In the Foundation Stage, we also encourage parents to share in the start of day activities with their children and use this opportunity to talk informally with them about our expectations and approaches to learning. This contact continues informally in Years 1 and 2 at the beginning and end of the school day when our teachers are available to chat.

In addition, we have adopted a middle management structure that uses Phase Coordinators instead of Subject Coordinators, and have chosen to combine our Foundation Stage and Key Stage 1 under one Phase Coordinator in order to ensure a better overview in terms of curriculum coverage, consistency of approach and monitoring of progression. Once a fortnight the Phase Coordinator meets with all staff working in his or her Phase and this regular discussion time ensures ideas are shared and implemented across the age range. In addition, the Phase Coordinator is given cover time to visit and monitor the various classes within his or her Phase

Within Foundation and Key Stage 1, children are used to working in groups, either independently or with the teacher. They enjoy participating in the various activities organised around a particular theme and the role of talk, often in a range of languages between peers is, I believe, what helps to cement the learning. Whether adult-led, adult-guided or child initiated, learning through play activities really works here, because it provides a meaningful context and purpose for the children to practise skills they either already know, or are becoming familiar with. Indeed, through play I believe children have the best opportunities for discovery learning too.

For example, just before Christmas our reception class were developing skills within the theme of 'Christmas Preparations'. With the teaching assistant fully involved in the planning, the teacher provided a carousel of activities for the children to experience during the week, each one geared to developing a particular set of skills and 'learning muscles'. This detailed planning included a plan for the Outdoor Activities, outlined below, to extend the learning through play. There was a Santa's workshop for wrapping presents, Christmas card & Santa letter writing, dressing the Christmas tree and filling a Christmas stocking. Within this framework, I was able to observe a significant number of learning experiences, which were generated by the children themselves whilst involved in their structured play activities. One group of three girls I saw eagerly supported each other in sounding out letters to form their message for a Christmas card. Once the cards were written, they watched each other and talked through the process of slipping them into the right sized envelope, sticking the envelope down and writing a name on the front before posting it in the Post Box. This was an act of real collaboration, involving self-help and perseverance in navigating what was a new experience for most of the children involved.

Our reception children experience a 'gentle transition' into Year 1 where they are able to continue and identify with activities and settings that are familiar to them from their reception year. The Indoor and Outdoor Learning environment in Year 1 is set up to include the Early Learning areas of sand and water play, a role play area, a writing area, and a construction and painting area. Year 1 also embrace 'Rise and Shine' workbook activities at the start of the day which are designed to hone fine motor skills, as well as structured play activities that sit alongside adult and teacher-led activities during the Literacy and Numeracy sessions. Peer group learning opportunities from the Foundation Stage are continued into Year 1 and 2, when once a week on 'Discovery Day' both Year 1 and 2 amalgamate into mixed ability vertical age groups that work together on the current theme and planned activities aimed at supporting skills learning.

In conclusion, I feel that strong leadership, an ability to promote change through discussion and good role-modelling are essential in ensuring that all staff feel able to take on new approaches, and incorporate play into their teaching. However, for indoors and outdoors play to be meaningfully integrated into the school's pedagogical approach it is necessary to ensure that structures are in place to support it. In this piece, I hope that I have highlighted the importance of developing a curriculum that includes opportunities for play, providing physical spaces for children to play in and adapting management structures in order to facilitate cooperation and encourage continuity. Of course, the willingness and flexibility of staff to adopt change and sensitively evaluate the success of new approaches is invaluable. As Head, I have the responsibility to create an atmosphere within the school that encourages the free exchange of ideas and opinions in order for teaching and learning to develop in the best interests of the child.

There is always more to do in ensuring we capitalise on our childrens' exceptional learning ability in these early years, providing them with activities that are in tune with the way they learn most effectively through play and collaborative talk. This has to be the way forward and as a school, we continue to plan our teaching and learning with this in mind.

Weekly Planning for the outdoor area in the Early Years Foundation Stage

	Writing area	Chalk board	Water/Messy play	Construction	Role play	Creative
Areas of Learning	L, PD, CL,	L, CL, MD, PSE, EAD	KUW, PSE	PSE, KUW, EAD, PD	KUW, PD, PSE, CL	EAD, PD
Characteristics of Effective Learning	Being involved and concentrating	Choosing ways to do things Playing with what they know	Finding out and exploring Being involved and concentrating	Having their own ideas Making links Choosing ways to do things Being willing to 'have a go'	Having their own ideas Making links Choosing ways to do things Being involved and concentrating Playing with what they know	Choosing ways to do things Having their own ideas Making links
Learning Muscles	Reciprocity Imitation	Reciprocity Collaboration	Resilience Noticing	Reflectiveness Planning Revising	Resilience Absorption- state of flow Perseverance	Resourcefulness Making Links
Structured Activities to take place throughout the week	Writing letters to Santa Post box, letters, writing implements, key words, example letters Table needed Jolly postman, bike, letter bag, postman costume	Large Christmas tree in green card on chalk board with a selection of crayons, felt pens, for children to decorate with mark making, Circle shapes for children to stick on tree and decorate	Santa slime, red slime with glitter In green water tray. Jelly bath with red food colouring, red and green glitter, cinnamon and ginger spices	Santa's workshop Building toys. Selection of small construction equipment Tools, elves ears, large ears on a red or green band.	Santa's present wrapping station. Christmas hat, selection of toys, wrapping paper, gift tags, ribbon, boxes, sellotape, scissors, Santa sacks, Santa hats	Printing wrapping paper using Christmas sponges Easels

Chris Williams

Chris Williams is Headteacher of St George's La Storta Junior School in Rome, and has always worked in international schools. Her Masters Degree in Education enabled her to develop her keen interest in understanding how children learn, and she continually strives to achieve the best opportunities for learning within the school setting.

When play is a foreign language: transformation of the early years learning environment

Audrey Dralega, Primary Head Teacher, Rainbow International School, Kampala, Uganda

The nature of the problem should have been apparent as I stood gazing at the 5m long climb-on pirate ship which we had finally completed in the playground. It was a real feat of engineering; built into the bank of our playground space to conserve the very limited open space available to the children. The pirate ship represented collaboration between a small and enthusiastic team of parents; one of whom supplied the engineering know-how, the other two being 'outdoor architects'. My part in the project was ensuring full play value in the design and the tight over sight of safety issues.

Built on two levels with a slatted bridge and block and galley ladders, the ship was carefully planned to give opportunities to use a variety of large motor skills and to exercise imaginative play opportunities. It had taken almost a year in the planning.

Now it was finally complete, it needed to be 'launched'!

Having recently returned from a holiday in Jamaica with the vivid story of Port Royal and Lord Nelson still bubbling in my imagination, I stood before the ship, contemplating a first school assembly in which I would surprise the children by dressing up as Blackbeard, hoisting the skull and crossbones on our rather impressive mast and spinning a magical tale of adventure on the high seas - imagination, adventure, physical challenge and history brought to life. I couldn't wait!

But then it happened - the parent sidled up to me and also gazed at our magnificent ship in silent contemplation.

'Wow, that's great!' he said. 'What is it for?'

For? Indeed, the purpose of play and the question of 'what it is for' is the subject of this case study.

One of the main challenges we faced as a school was the dichotomy between the vision of effective primary education held by the school leadership, and the perception of a significant number of the parent body and teaching staff.

Based in East Africa, the lively and creative international school, for which I am primary Head Teacher, draws around 65% of its children and staff from the region and a significant number from South Asia. The school follows the National Curriculum for England and is committed to gaining full accreditation with the Council for British International Schools (COBIS) under the standards for British Schools Overseas. However, when I joined the school we had a substantial number of parents and teaching staff who viewed a good education as involving a lot of studious listening and copious amounts of written work. Most parents choose the school as a strong alternative to the national system, which is characterised by extremely long hours, a prescriptive curriculum, great emphasis on rote learning and the exact recall of facts. Yet, changing views on how young children learn best was one of our main tasks and one which we have approached systematically over a period of years.

The pirate ship conversation illustrated to me that we were indeed involved in a process not too dissimilar to speaking a foreign language to unfamiliar ears. Attitudinal change, of both parents and teachers and raising teachers understanding of the content and rationale of the primary curriculum, were the main areas to be addressed.

It was a process which was time consuming and at times exasperating, but very much worthwhile in terms of the development of the teaching team and, most importantly, in terms of the enrichment of the children's learning environment and raising standards. We were looking to obtain buy-in from all areas of the school community and this would take persistence and a clear understanding of leading sustained change.

The shaping of the teachers' thinking and attitudes has been the focus for many studies and applied strategies. In this particular context I worked on one aspect which I would express as *benefit or value*. If we could help teachers to see the direct and peripheral benefits of using the new teaching methods, there would be a much greater chance of enthusiastic pursuit of change, rather than the begrudging reluctance that so often accompanied educational innovation.

Thus, emphasis was placed on both clarity of purpose and on supporting teachers' individual aims and ambitions; the teacher's desire to improve practice, thereby becoming more effective and therefore more marketable. Now some purists might question this approach on the basis that it can seem a little narcissistic to show enthusiasm only when direct benefit is perceived, but I hold to the view that the individual ambitions of the teacher should not be seen as separate to the progress of the school – indeed my role as Headteacher is to develop the individual within the on-going development of the school, giving opportunities to try new things and discover strengths as well as contributing existing skills. Should a teacher both understand the rationale and perceive benefit, this can act as a powerful spur to action. Instead of simply presenting educators with the instructions and directives (the 'what'), I would provide them with the rationale (the 'why').

This question needed us to explore how children learn.

Through staff meetings and training days, we started with our common experiences of babies and young children; we explored the nature of early learning starting with how children acquire language – a fascinating journey from pre-birth to three or four years. This opened up a whole new level of understanding of the child's developing mind. Meetings were held with parents to inform them about the changes of approach and to generally raise their awareness and understanding. As a result, teachers – and parents who attended the meetings – could more easily make the connection between their own experience of the young child, and the need to provide a language-rich environment and to extend a child's range of language uses. Importantly, this approach enriched the understanding of the young child as a rational and active learner, with a natural ability for quite high level reasoning, enabling them to process a series of random sentences (data), and from this cacophony of sound, identify grammatical patterns which they then try out. For example, we looked at the amazing ability of the two year old to figure out grammatical rules such as 'the past tense of a verb often ends with /ed/'. So the child may say 'he runned away'. We all know that the child did not hear that from an adult -or at least we hope they did not! The child cannot express the hypothesis, but she can use it! Not only does the child use the language pattern they have perceived, but by the age of four can usually generate an enormous range of utterances – many of which are grammatically correct.

We also considered the development of mathematical thinking – the idea that babies are naturally inclined, even 'hard-wired' to look for and identify pattern. We examined the idea that in play, babies and young children are exploring a series of patterns and hypotheses.

This level of understanding opened up the mind of the teachers. They saw children differently and many teachers became more interested in figuring out how they might better support this amazing process. And the direct benefit to the teacher? Effectiveness in practice and, with it came greater job satisfaction.

The introduction of continuous provision in Early Years Foundation Stage (EYFS) was the next natural step, but this seemed to be taking a very long time to be understood and implemented by the teachers. It took observation and discussion to begin to identify the reason for this intransigence. Teachers were afraid that more play was equal to less teaching and therefore less learning. They were unclear about how play could be useful - enjoyable, certainly – but there was apprehension about whether play could actually really lead to high level learning.

My periodic incursions into the EYFS classrooms were never going to be adequate. Staff would politely do as directed, but within weeks would go back to the practices of extended time on the mat and activities that practiced rudimentary motor skills, such as letter formation, of limited learning value. The children were still compliant, but it was clear that the limited or non-existent choice and self direction was limiting their growth and development as individuals.

More radical action was needed and it took three approaches. The first was recruiting a lead practitioner who had strong inter-personal skills and, importantly, a real passion for early years education. We were fortunate in that the teacher identified had arrived from a good quality EYFS practice environment in which the school had achieved the outstanding grade at inspection. The effect of a high energy, creative practitioner was immediate, though not without pockets of resistance. While the staff related to her very well, some had never seen effective practice in terms of children having continuous provision and so the teachers were still anxious about letting go and effectively becoming the children's resource.

The second approach was therefore to send two teachers to the UK to attend a three day course which included rigorous coverage of the content and rationale of the EYFS curriculum, but also importantly included visits to outstanding UK schools. The teachers were tasked to look at the levels of attainment, record keeping and how teaching staff engage with the children. This approach was quite effective in terms of the teachers returning and implementing changes to set up and the all-important mindset change, but it was apparent that the majority of staff would never have a similar opportunity, simply due to budget constraints.

The third strategy, involved inviting in an expert trainer I had encountered whilst on a course on best practice in Early Years. At the course in London the delivery and content were so clear, innovative and inspirational, that I immediately invited the consultant to come to Kampala to deliver training, not just to my staff, but to teachers and teaching assistants from all interested schools in the East Africa region. Organised with COBIS, the course focus was on teachers and teaching assistants recognising teachable moments and supporting and extending learning therein. The course attracted participants from nine international schools in the city and further afield and included teachers, support staff and a school director. The most rewarding aspects of this arrangement were that teachers were able to engage with other practitioners from a wide range of schools, discuss good practice and their progress towards improving their own practice. It also meant that across the city, the general level of provision was spurred to improve.

A parent meeting was held with the same visiting trainer, which was well attended by a range of parents from the participating schools. Entitled 'How Parents can Support Effective Learning', the meeting focused on learning through play. Parents have also been invited to open afternoons to join their children at play.

The process of teaching 'the language of play' is by no means complete, but it is certainly well underway. Children's ability to make choices and apply their learning has shown significant improvement over the past -two years. Reception age children are now regularly choosing to write and often write for a purpose - for example making lists or invitations to events. Continuous provision and observing children at play are now embedded practice. There is still work to do in ensuring all children engage and show signs of deep level involvement. The focus continues to be on supporting assistants to understand how to extend and enrich a child's language use or understanding of mathematical concepts.

We have noted real changes in attitudes. The children are keener to come to school and both parents and teachers are seeing that children do indeed learn through play. Most importantly of all, however, is the realisation of both teachers and parents, that their understanding of children's play and the quality adult-child interaction is absolutely crucial to this process.

Audrey Dralega

Audrey Dralega is currently the Primary Head Teacher of Rainbow International School, Uganda. Prior to relocating to Uganda, Audrey served as an independent consultant and Course Tutor in the School of Education, University of Leeds, UK, where she taught the Primary Mathematics component of the Post Graduate Certificate in Education (PGCE). She has also delivered numerous college training courses on

Early Childhood Learning, Special Educational Needs and teaching methods for the international curriculum. She has led numerous courses for serving teachers and specializes in Mathematical Thinking and Early Years Education.

All change! The transformation of early years learning

Jemo Ergen EYFS Co-ordinator, Rainbow International School, Kampala, Uganda

Rainbow International School is a private school based in Kampala, Uganda. It opened in 1991 with only 29 children. The school now has approximately 800 students on roll and runs from Nursery to Year 13. It is split into two sections: Primary and Secondary. It offers the National Curriculum of England (NC) throughout. In the Primary section of the school the content of the NC is delivered through the International Primary Curriculum (IPC), the Cambridge International Primary Programme (CIPP) and the Early Years Foundation Stage Curriculum (EYFS).

The school is a member of the Council of British International Schools (COBIS) and is also registered with the Department for Education (DfE) in the UK. The children from Nursery to Year 13 take part in events and competitions organised by COBIS such as art, science and poetry competitions and also sporting events such as the COBIS Games. The school also offers the children the opportunity to complete the Duke of Edinburgh Awards. The involvement of the children in a range of extra-curricular activities is seen as an essential part of the students' individual development.

There are four departments in the Primary school: Early Years, Key Stage 1, Key Stage 2 and Special Educational Needs (SEN). The Early Years Department consists of four classes: Nursery, Kindergarten and two reception classes. From Year 1 upwards there are three classes per year group. The SEN department works with groups of and individual children to support their learning. Where possible the school aims to provide children with in-class support. They also offer support for children who have English as an Additional Language (EAL). Rainbow International School offers small class sizes with a good adult to child ratio throughout the school in order to offer a holistic education that encourages the development of each student. The school is co-educational and is extremely diverse culturally. There are children from approximately 60 different nationalities attending the school. The staff members at the school also come from around the world and it is this multicultural atmosphere that makes Rainbow International School a special place.

In the Early Years Department at Rainbow International School we follow the Early Years Foundation Stage Curriculum (September 2013.) Children are offered a range of activities, both indoors and outdoors, that stimulate learning through play. Adults in the early years scaffold the children's learning through talk, modelling and open ended questioning. Children's progress is closely tracked using a profile/learning journey and the adults facilitate progress by challenging the children and taking them to the next step on a much individualised basis.

The Early Years Department has been on a long journey of development over a period of many years. Since beginning my work in January 2014, there have been many changes to the Early Years Department at Rainbow. In making these necessary changes we faced several challenges.

The staff in our setting are primarily local Ugandans, as is the case in many international schools and therefore, staff often have no direct experience working within the British system. The Ugandan education system is extremely different to that in Rainbow International School. Children are often in very large classes and the general view in Uganda is that 'teachers teach and children learn.' Learning by repetition and rote is standard practice. Although at Rainbow teachers were eager to learn and try something new, 'old habits die hard.' Commonly the only experience that teachers have is their own education within a very rigid system and teacher training that prepared them to teach within the very same system. Despite this there were many elements of good practice: the staff had good relationships with children and were keen to ensure progress; there were elements of play within the classrooms; the outdoor area was equipped with a climbing area and the classrooms were fairly well resourced.

There was a need to introduce and support the teaching and support staff methods, strategies and systems that are viewed as 'good practice' in the UK system. Little did I know the difficulties that this would pose. This has been most challenging aspect to tackle; changing people's mindset. "Play is the highest form of research" said Albert Einstein and I had to show my staff that this was true. Definitely the biggest and most significant change to our department has been the change of views in terms of *how* children learn. The staff now see, understand and most importantly, believe in the value of play. The children are more relaxed and are engaged in continuous provision that is well organised. The children learn more easily and are eager to be involved in activities with their peers. They accept and appreciate adult interaction because they view the adults input as joining in with their play rather than 'work' that must be completed. We are now able to extend the children's learning further and in a more cross-curricular way as the adults are "down on the children's level."

Over the past year and a half we have invested a lot of time, effort and money into training our staff. We have tackled areas of provision within the classroom such as small world and play dough as well as children's development with regards to gross and fine motor skills, reading and writing. Of course, we also looked at assessment strategies and developed our new profile in order to track children's progress. Due to improved understanding there was a noticeable improvement in teaching and this is having an impact on learning. The interactions that occur between the adults and the children are more meaningful and as the adults are able to draw on their knowledge of the stages of development that children go through they are able to support the children's learning appropriately.

The organisation of space became an important consideration. Nursery and Kindergarten previously used separate areas of one large classroom and had a veranda area in front of the classroom that was unused. We reorganised the classroom and veranda into one large classroom and set up areas that are essential to create an excellent learning environment in early years. Children in our setting now have access to play dough, water, sand, painting, mathematical activities writing and mark-making, reading, construction, small world, role play, computer, fine motor and creative areas. They also have free access to the outdoor area all day instead of having fixed 'play times.' Learning takes place all of the time and in all of the areas and learning opportunities are maximised no matter where the children choose to play.

As I previously mentioned, the introduction of the concept of continuous provision was an important process. With the change in curriculum, a renewed understanding of how children learn, new areas in the classroom and a free flow environment, the children are able to move around the classroom and engage in activities that are of interest to them. This initially raised worries of "but how will they learn anything?" and has been our main priority throughout. Through training and practise the staff have gained confidence and the children have most definitely shown us that this method is effective. Children are confident, independent and happy. They are engaged and as we work with them we can see that learning is happening **all the time**.

In order to increase learning opportunities resources needed renewing and replenishing in many areas and although the classrooms were well resourced with construction toys, board games, puzzles and other 'catalogue' resources it was clear that there was a need for more in order to create opportunities for children to be creative. Again, there was a mind-set that needed to be overcome. By placing scissors and real knives in the play dough area staff's perceptions were challenged and they would tell you that these changes scared them initially. Mostly staff were concerned about safety and children hurting themselves. When they saw that children were more engaged and concentrated harder while playing (as they needed to ensure they didn't cut themselves) they opened their minds up to the possibilities that could be created. Since then we have ordered tyres, crates, planks of wood, bamboo channelling, large basins, umbrellas, large sheets of material and balls for our outdoor area. For play dough we have ordered resources such as (real) rolling pins, chopping boards, knives and the list goes on. In short, we have tried to resource our classrooms and outdoor area with resources that are 'flexible' and support open ended play. By this, I mean resources that offer a variety of uses. Tyres and crates can be used for balancing, to build a den or a car or to create a road for the bikes, just to name a few. It is essential to remember that children are imaginative and creative and will often find more and better uses for things than we can as adults. Not only do we buy local resources (such as the resources mentioned above) but we recycle **everything**! Parents, staff and children drop off boxes, clothes, material, bottles, bottle lids and we put them all to good use. Overall, many significant changes have been made: curriculum, timetables, resources, teaching style, classroom set up and every good practitioner realises that improvement is a continuing daily process.

The effectiveness of practice can only be truly judged by one thing: the children's attainment. We are still in the early stages of this change in system (of teaching and assessment) so it will take a few years of assessing children's attainment against the early learning goals to see the overall measures of progress but by the end of this year the improvements in children's attainment will be clearer to us. We project that at least 70% of the children will achieve the expected levels with 10% exceeding the early learning goals.

As statistical data on end of year results is not yet available to us we have to use other methods to judge our effectiveness. We look at the interactions between the children and the adults, the progress that takes place during an interaction, the views of the parents and we track the children's progress in their individual profiles. So far, all of the above methods show us that our children are making good progress and we believe that this system benefits the lower ability child as they are more likely to succeed in a low pressure, nurturing environment. The children are excited to be involved in the new learning experiences that are continually on offer. It has also been noted by other teachers and parents that the children are more eager to come to school and are excited to learn.

We are looking forwards and have a clear action plan for the year. We will continue to work on our previous changes in order to ensure consistency and continuity as well as tackling other areas. Our main areas for development for the remainder of this year are assessment, outdoor learning, child initiated learning and parent partnership. There is always lots to think about.

Jemo Ergen

Jemo Ergen trained as a teacher at the University of Wales, Newport, United Kingdom. She qualified with Physical Education as her specialism but has since found that her niche is in early years. She taught in Wales for three years and then moved to Ras Al Khaimah (UAE) where she taught for four years. She now lives in Kampala, Uganda and works at Rainbow International School Uganda as a reception class teacher and Early Years Co-ordinator

Making sure learning happens in foundation stage physical education

Joanne Marshall, teacher at an international primary school in Brunei.

This case study describes part of my teaching experience in a large, international school in Qatar. The primary school was situated on a closed community, which housed in the region of 12,000 people. Approximately 85% of pupils at the school lived on the community complex and all their parents worked for the same Qatari company. The other 15% of the pupils were local Qatari children and children whose parents worked at the school.

The Primary School catered for approximately 1,650 children from Early Years Foundation Stage (EYFS) to Year 6. Students came from all over the world, but the largest groups were from Malaysia, Qatar, Indonesia, Pakistan, Algeria, Philippines and Egypt. Approximately 90% of the children spoke English as an Additional Language (EAL).

There were 11 EYFS classes, each with between 19 and 22 children in them, and they followed the Early Years Foundation Stage (EYFS) curriculum of England four to five year olds. Every class had a full time teaching assistant (TA) who supported the children learning in class and in specialist lessons. Most children in EYFS had received some preschool education before starting, but at least 10% of the children had not had any formal education before arriving at the school. This combined with the fact that a number of the children had no spoken English, made communication for the class teacher and specialist teachers difficult.

The use of talk partners (TP), peer assessment and a greater focus on children creating their own success criteria was introduced in the 2013/14 academic year and all teachers in the primary school were expected to be implementing these in their day-to-day lessons.

All Infant School children had two 40-minute Physical Education (PE) lessons a week and these were taught by a specialist PE teacher. The infant PE curriculum had been developed by the school and was predominately skills based. It consisted of half termly units as outlined in the table below.

Term	Activities
Term 1	Fun- skills
	Multi- skills Ball
Term 2	Gymnastics
	Games
Term 3	Swimming
	Outdoor Adventurous Activities (OAA), skills and problem solving

As there were 11 EYFS classes to teach, these units could be taught in any order depending on the class and availability of space in the school.

The EYFS class described in this case study consisted of 19 children (11 boys and 8 girls) aged between four and five. All of the children were EAL, three children had no schooling prior to starting EYFS and there was an autistic boy who only attended school for three hours a day and was provided with 1:1 support. The PE unit undertaken was 'Multi-skills ball' and although this says ball it also include of hoops and quoits. The focus was to develop childrens hand eye coordination through rolling, hitting, kicking, throwing and catching skills using a wide range of balls and other equipment.

Meetings with the teacher were undertaken in order, where possible, to link classroom learning with PE. Also, the skills taught in PE lessons directly link to the physical development (PD) aspect of the EYFS so these feedback sessions helped the class teacher with future planning and assessment of PD in the class.

At the beginning of the 'Multi-skills' unit the children were provided with a selection of various sized balls, hoops, quoits, bats *etc.* and a large enough space for them to explore the equipment through play. This lesson was child initiated and, although the PE teacher and TA were in the room and interacted with the children, the main purpose of activity was to observe and assess, by using the support of photographs and videos, what skills the children already had, what they did with the equipment and how they interacted and communicated with the other children; starting the assessment planning cycle below.

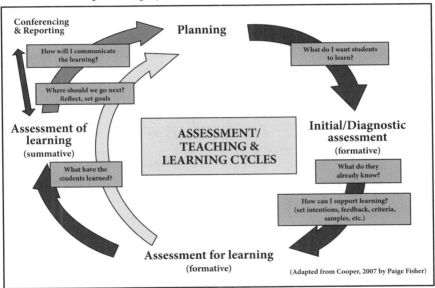

Using this information the PE teacher could identify next steps for individuals in the class and plan the next lesson in order to develop their skills in the specific focus area. The lesson could then be adapted to suit the needs of the children.

During this activity:

- A group of four girls decided to sit in a circle and roll a large ball to each other.

- A group of boys and girls played together with the hoops jumping through them, playing hoopla, joining them together to make a chain or rolling them.

- Three boys spent most of the lesson bouncing balls and trying to score goals in the basketball hoops.

- A group of four boys spent most of the lesson kicking a football against the wall or to a friend. Most of these could also stop a moving ball.

This demonstrated that a number of children were comfortable playing with a range of different equipment, could cooperate with others and were already developing good ball skills and hand-eye coordination.

However, three children did not cope so well with the activity:

- The autistic boy would only play with equipment that was blue and got very upset and disruptive. He was also sometimes aggressive towards others if someone took the blue equipment away from him or he was given equipment that was not blue.

In all the lessons following this we made sure that he always had access to blue equipment.

- Two children, a boy and a girl, did not participate at all. The boy refused to participate in the activity and could not communicate his reasons why. The girl just walked around the play area crying, but she did not interact with anyone or pick up any of the equipment. She was also not able to communicate why.

The teacher was notified and was able to ascertain, from talking to these children and their parents. The girl was afraid of the balls especially the larger ones. Both the boy and the girl found the openness of this session quite scary there was too much equipment and too many children just doing what they wanted. These children preferred a little more structure. Therefore, provisions were made for them in subsequent lesson until they were more comfortable participating in the activities.

At the end of the initial lesson the children were asked to sit with their talk partner and tell them what they enjoyed the best, what they thought they were good at and what they wanted to be better at. One of the problems of working with young children, particularly in an international school, is that of communication. Some of them have little or no English and sometimes find even expressing themselves in their home language difficult.

Following this initial lesson and observations the next two lessons were planned based on the children's needs and focused on the skill of catching.

Lesson two comprised of three activities for the children to participate in and the class was split into three groups. I have found that younger children tend to lose focus and become bored quite quickly, so by providing shorter activities the children should stay motivated, interested and on task. Two of the activities were also differentiated, according to the children's individual needs, and were led by the specialist PE teacher and the TA. The third activity was free play with a given set of equipment.

To maximize the children's learning, the PE teacher modelled the adult led activities so the children were able to see what was expected of them. This is particularly useful for those children who do not speak or understand English, as it is visual. In order to create success criteria (SC) for catching, the children observed the PE teacher making silly mistakes *eg* not looking at the ball, having their hands in their pockets etc. This made it fun, but also allowed the children to correct the teacher and come up with a set of SC that they could follow in order to catch correctly themselves. Therefore, they were actually using the SC to help the teacher succeed and this in turn developed their understanding of the skill. Pictures of the SC (ready position, hands ready to receive the ball, eye on the ball) were used as a visual representation to refer to during the lesson.

This meant the information had been presented in a variety of ways (visual, audio and kinesthetic) therefore, making it accessible to all the children and maximizing pupil learning.

The TA activity involved the children working individually to throw a ball up and catch it. The size of the ball and material varied according to their ability. The TA was able to guide the children and observe their achievements, which was disseminated to the PE teacher at the end of the lesson.

The teacher led activity involved children throwing and catching balls with a partner. The SC was revised and some of the children identified that the person throwing the ball needed to do it successfully so the other person could catch correctly. In their pairs they had to try and remind each other how to catch correctly therefore adding peer assessment into the activity. If they achieved the task correctly they could 'high five' with their partner. The activity was differentiated by the distance the children were apart and also the size of ball that they were catching. Each group had a chance to participate in all the activities and at the end of the lesson they worked with their TP again to explain what they had learnt and how they felt they had done. They found this quite hard but did refer to the pictures of the success criteria and also actions.

After evaluating this lesson the next two lessons were planned. They included challenges for the more able children and reinforcement activities for those who struggled. Therefore providing every child with their next steps and ensuring that learning was focused to individual needs.

I feel that using assessment and regular communication with the class teacher and TA to inform my planning ensured that children were provided with challenging learning objectives and a very clear success criteria, which in turn impacted on the childrens learning. I also feel that children communication is important as it helps them to become more proactive and reflective learners.

Communication is the biggest barrier with EYFS children, especially in an international school such as this one, where EAL numbers are very high. However, one of the advantages with PE is its practical nature and instructions can be provided visually and verbally, therefore making it a lot more accessible. Children can also achieve and make progress at their own level in a lesson. I think asking the children what they want to learn in a PE unit would be a useful exercise and would give them more ownership of the lesson, however the issue of communication would probably come up again with so many EAL children in the class.

I also feel that making better links to the learning going on in a FS classroom would be beneficial as it would make PE lessons an extension of the classroom. This, in turn, could provide useful feedback for both the specialist teacher and the class teacher and therefore, be used to inform future planning. This would ensure every pupil is provided with a range of learning opportunities.

Joanne Marshall

Joanne Marshall is currently teaching at an international primary school in Brunei. She has a Masters Degree in International Education from The University of Bath and has a real interest in the development and implementation of the International Primary Curriculum (IPC) both in the UK and internationally. For the past 18 years she has been a class teacher, subject coordinator and year leader in schools in the UK, Saudi Arabia and Qatar. She has also been a specialist Primary Physical Education (PE) teacher and has taught PE including swimming to children from Foundation Stage (FS) to Year 6.

'Is this really teaching?' - The role of the adult in supporting learning

Helen Stevens, Assistant Head Primary, British School Bucharest, Romania

The British School of Bucharest (BSB) is celebrating its 15th year of offering a British education to a variety of different nationalities living in and around Bucharest. The British School has children from over 50 countries enrolled; with around 25% being native English speakers. The school was born out of one parent's desire to find the perfect school for her son; one which allowed for creativity and independence alongside a rounded curriculum. The school opened with only seven children and has since continued to grow into a community with over 500; ranging in ages from 12 months to 18 years old. The BSB offers a creative and developmental curriculum that is also in line with the National Curriculum of England requirements. We offer all students from early years to secondary the chance to learn a broad range of subjects; with a strong emphasis on English and mathematics. Our school aims to provide children with the opportunities they need to grow into strong, independent, inquisitive and creative thinkers. Our role as educators and the way that we interact with our children is the key to ensuring that we fulfil the aims we have for the children at our school.

Our Early Years Foundation Stage (EYFS) department is made up of a 'crib and crèche' class, two pre-school classes and two reception classes. Our crib, crèche and pre-school classes all have one teacher and two teaching assistants. Our reception classes have one teacher and one teaching assistant per class. For pre-school our class sizes are capped at 16 and within reception at 18. The EYFS department is split between two buildings but all within one campus. Both buildings offer children access to outdoor learning provision.

'Is this really teaching?' There is still a widespread view that the life of an early years teacher involves days of playing. The view that playing is not learning can sometimes be a difficult opinion to shake, especially within the international school sector where opinions on previous educational experiences may not match what we practice. Our school states we follow the National Curriculum for England (including the Early Years Foundation Stage) for early years and play based learning forms the basis of this. Young children learn from investigating the mud kitchen to spending quality time outside in various weathers and lots more besides. The role of the teacher and teaching assistant may seem to others that they are watching children just 'play' and it is questioned how can this be defined as 'teaching'. The question then has to be asked what one defines as 'teaching'.

At our school, through three way teacher observations and class twinning we have tried to dismiss the 'EYFS play' myth. This has helped to raise the profile of our EYFS teachers and to demonstrate the many teaching roles they have throughout the day. Here at the BSB we would define the role of our early years teachers as constantly striving to allow children to realise their capabilities. We do this through carefully modelling and scaffolding the learning of all children. Teachers work together to provide opportunities for the children to take ownership of their learning journey, and adapt and develop opportunities for children to engage with their own interests in a productive and effective manner which is meaningful to their own development. Basically when we see what our children are interested in then we develop that curiosity. It can be from the truly elaborate to the very simple; one of our reception teachers noticed that her class wanted to constantly dress up in pieces of fabric that were about her classroom. The teacher saw this as a wonderful opportunity for imaginative play and an area for discussion. The following day she collected all the materials she could find and left it within her role play corner. The children in the class spent the day dressed in outfits they had created; eating snacks, playing in them and thoroughly enjoying the experience.

Michael Rosen has said 'It may seem an obvious thing to say, but one of the best things we can do with young children is to have interesting and enjoyable conversations with them.' Just this kind of opportunity arose from play with fabric. This activity allowed the teacher the opportunity to develop her children's language skills. She was able to ask the children questions about their costumes; she encouraged them to interact with each other initiating scenarios where the characters might meet and the stories were shared as a class. To an outsider this may seem a 'nice' activity but the class teacher recognised this as an excellent opportunity for the development of language, with speaking and listening opportunities and collaborative work between the children. Being in an international setting the importance of giving our children interesting opportunities to develop their language skills is vital. Added to this, as teaching is through the medium of English there has to be engaging and stimulating discussion opportunities within our classrooms to use and to enjoy a language other than mother tongue.

The importance of language acquisition and the teacher's role in allowing children opportunities to develop was recently highlighted in one of our preschool classes. The child's first language was not English and the child felt very uncomfortable within an English speaking setting. One of the roles of the adult in the first few weeks was first to offer comfort and emotional support alongside being an educator. All young children can find walking into a new environment a daunting experience but within our international setting this can be even more with a new language to learn too. The role of the teacher here is vital to ensuring the child feels comfortable and happy to come to school. Within a few weeks this preschool child had settled well into her classroom and was actively involved in learning activities. During the daily shared reading activity the teaching assistant invited the child to listen and participate. The teacher modelled reading the book; holding it correctly and she asked the children questions to aid discussion, 'What is the monkey doing? What do you think the Mummy said when the monkey bumped his head?' They sat listening to the story, focussing on the pictures and discussing the 'five little monkeys'.

Through teachers modelling book skills and techniques children naturally copy this within their own play. Often re-enacting these teacher led scenarios around the classroom during their independent time. In this example the class teacher noted the interest in the story and the accompanying song was sung together in the classroom. Modelling to the class the actions that accompanied the song the children were all able to follow and join in. This resulted in the child taking it upon herself to create her own area in which she could happily sing about five little monkeys. She collected five small world people and placed them on the table. After this she began singing the song that she has heard and somewhat memorised and was able to remove the people one by one after they had jumped on the bed. Other children then came to join her and the teaching assistant encouraged them to join in too. The teaching assistant that had shared the story with her just sat and listened to her singing; then used the iPad to record the activity for the child's assessment. When the child had finished singing the assistant encouraged her to develop her ideas through questioning, 'What other animals could we sing about?', 'How did the monkeys hurt themselves?', 'Shall we be the little monkeys?'

It was interesting to observe that the teaching assistant kept a distance when the girl was singing, allowing the child to develop her own ideas. This is very important and staff within the EYFS setting recognise when it is beneficial to step in and when they need to allow children the space to follow their own thinking. This is an area, which on occasion staff may need to be reminded about, as it is easy to want to overly guide an activity in the way you have planned it.

Over the past year, our school has been working through a programme for developing outstanding teaching. Each week teachers throughout the school are encouraged to reflect on their everyday practice and focus on the nine areas that the programme identifies as leading the way to exceptional teaching. Week nine was titled, 'Get the hell out'. The programme stated that 'Getting out of the way' is, "all about the teacher not being the bottleneck, not trying to control the outcomes, not trying to guide students towards a particular answer, not leading them towards your understanding of the world. Rather, it is all about realising that they are capable of literally astonishing accomplishments once you let them learn what they want and customise how they want to learn it."

Recently one of our reception teachers spoke about remembering to take a step back and making sure not to overly lead the activity. The children had recently studied 'Space' and the teacher had initiated a discussion around what food the children would take with them. The children did not respond straightaway to her questions so she was about to jump in with a list of questions and a possible solution; even beginning to bend down to gather some stones to use as 'food'. At that moment the children rushed off to gather chunks of ice and started telling the teacher about how this could be food. This led to a discussion about ice and its properties along with life in space. When speaking with the teacher she remarked how she felt her role had been to initiate the conversation and guide the children but equally how important it was to allow 'thinking time' in order for the children to further the activity independently. The teacher was then able to use this to discuss the qualities of melting and freezing and how this might affect their choice of food. Again the role of the teacher had been to plan an interesting topic but to not become too focussed on a particular outcome rather to allow the children the scope to explore. Early years teachers need to think on their feet at times and be prepared to go with the unexpected.

In conclusion here at BSB we are always displaying effective practice within the early years setting. We contribute daily to our children's wellbeing and care for their needs academically, emotionally and socially. We fully engage in all of their learning and develop this further with sensitivity. Each attribute the teacher holds can vary each day dependant on the child's interests and how we can see them develop academically. As a practitioner within the early years setting we are encouraged to find our own inner child to elaborate on how the children are thinking and seeing life itself. We find this helpful here at BSB in order to fulfil the needs of the children. Lots of situations are considered 'real life' in order to fulfil the children's learning potential both inside and outside of the classroom. There are always areas that we are developing and our most current being our outside learning environment and establishing how we wish to see this move forward. At our school we place our children's development, academic and creative opportunities at the forefront of all we do and our roles as teachers are to ensure that this happens daily.

Note: Information about the outstanding teaching development used at BSB can be found at (http://djn2mgzx0uvlm.cloudfront.net/Guardian_RootRepository/Saras/ContentPackaging/UploadRepository/267439/75009f97641e4bb780bd0d48b30ba881/AFrameworkForExceptionalTeaching.pdf) [Accessed 28th March 2015]

Helen Stevens

Helen has been teaching for over 12 years mostly within the United Kingdom. Her love of travel has led her to look at working internationally and it is an experience which she loves. She joined the British School of Bucharest as a Year 1 teacher in 2008 and has not looked back. Presently she is the Assistant Head of Primary; a role which she is thoroughly enjoying. Helen works closely with the teaching assistants (TAs) in the school, building upon the knowledge and skills they gained as part of the Certificate for Teaching Assistants in an International Context (CTAIC) and helping them to put new ideas into working practice. The best use of TAs within the British School Bucharest is an area she will continue to develop.

The view from here: comments on parents perspectives for joining the early years centre

Lucinda Wiser, Coordinator for Teaching Excellence, The American School Foundation, Mexico City, Mexico

The role of play in a child's life seems to have been changing over the last 50 years. Gone are the days when children don't go to any kind of school until they are five. Gone are the days that parents tell children to "go outside and play" without a concern for their safety. Gone are the days when the primary group of friends is from the neighbourhood.

We are currently in a world where many believe the sooner children learn to read and know their basic number sense, the better it will be for children; so today many children go to school at four years old and often at three years old. International parents, as well as parents from Mexico often feel that they can't even send their children to a babysitter or the daycare; they need to be sent to school.

The American School Foundation, A.C. (ASF) was founded in the late 19th century when a group of American industrialists living in Mexico City started a kindergarten in the home of John R. Davis. Kindergartens were a new concept in American education at the time, and Mr. Davis invited his mother-in-law, Mrs. Bessie Files, who had recently completed her training in this innovative approach to the education of young children, to teach in this newly created private school. The first nine students to enroll in Mrs. Files' Kindergarten class on August 6, 1888, were children from American, Mexican and British families who wanted the best in modern education taught in English for their children. Today, ASF serves over 2,000 students from all over the world. We are a Global International Baccalaureate School, and follow the Common Core State Standards from the United States.

Our mission: The American School Foundation, A.C. is an academically rigorous, international, university preparatory school, which offers students from diverse backgrounds the best of American independent education. In all aspects of school life students are encouraged to love learning, live purposefully and to become responsible, contributing citizens of the world.

What about the teachers who are hired to teach our early childhood today? Many of our early childhood teachers were hired back in the day when the major purpose of going to kindergarten was to learn to play well with others, and this remains important. Now our teachers at ASF also have increasingly high standards they must measure and report on; Standards from the Common Core State Standards, as well as our Primary Years Program (PYP). These standards are the foundational skills for literacy and numeracy as well as the social skills children need to learn to do well in school and in life. Today a question one hears bantered about among parents and teachers is about how much play children need versus how much academic time they need. However, are these really two opposing points of view? Is play really the opposite of learning and school? What about all the research that we have about how play does teach children about social roles, responsibility, and independence? What about the current learning research that shows how effective games are in teaching academic content, as referenced in the current Horizon Report? How does one find the balance between fun play and serious learning? Are they really different? Doesn't the research in "flow" by Mihaly Csikszentmihalyi teach us that when we are really engaged, no matter how academic the activity, we feel a sense of joy and timelessness? This is a matter we need to think about because many of our students here are in school for three sometimes four years before they enter 1st grade (six/ seven years old). Parents and children are certainly entitled to outcomes with that investment.

The issue some of our parents are facing is that with all the structured activities that are scheduled in the life of their children, the children are not learning how to be creative with free time. The children come to adults saying, "I'm bored" and expect the parents, or teachers to entertain them. If adults structure all the time of children, children don't learn how to be independent and they don't learn how to do things for themselves. They also need to have time to just do nothing: to sit, to think, to wonder, and to daydream.

In international schools there is an additional dimension: language. We often find that in the life of a small child, language will not separate children from playing together. However, as the children grow older, language becomes a bigger barrier and so does participation in local sports of the host country. Sometimes children coming to a host country are excluded from play because they don't know how to play the popular local sport or game.

Because the structure of the family has changed, play has also changed. Our families live in a very densely populated area with no great outdoor areas to 'go play'. Although the weather in Mexico allows for more outdoor time, when they do go outside, it is with supervision, either a parent or more often a nanny. The children often don't know other neighbourhood children to play with, so they can feel isolated. 'Play dates' are common but playing with other children from school will usually require a huge commute to other parts of the city. This means that parents depend on schools to provide playtime with other children. Birthday parties also take on a huge role in international schools and class activities. They are the social events for children and their moms.

Play at home can mean playing with the nanny. The social structure between a nanny and a child can bring about interesting results. Children playing with the maid or nanny, don't have to play fair, after all, life really does revolve around them. The nanny is their employee. In addition, parents talk about their children adopting the values of the nanny, who is the child's friend, caretaker, person they spend a lot of time with.

The children at our school come here for a variety of reasons. In addition to coming to the school because we offer a high quality American Education, one reason to apply to the Early Childhood Center is to make sure the child has a spot by 1st grade (six/seven years). Children come to secure a place later on. Another reason is parents want meaningful activities for their children in English and they both work very long hours. A third reason to enroll in our Early Childhood Center is because parents want their children to acquire English. A reason to come to this school often is for the social connections the children make. In a culture that relies on relationships to get things done, play with the "right" people is hugely important to parents. Parents want their children to spend time with others with the same socio economic status, the future leaders of Mexico. By the 12th grade (17/18 years) this is a very tight group that will support our children with a lifetime of connections here in Mexico.

Of course these are my opinions, I am sure there are people who don't see things the way I do. I am a guest in this country.

Lucinda Wiser

Lucinda Wiser is currently working at The American School Foundation in Mexico City as the Coordinator for Teaching Excellence. She has worked at international private American Schools in Syria, Pakistan, Guatemala, Mexico and Venezuela, as well as working in Washington and Utah State in the public school system. Her educational career includes teaching Preschool - 12th grade, administration, instructional coaching, and consulting. She was also the supervisor for Washington Reading Corps of Eastern Washington.

Not stuck indoors: challenges to outdoor provision in a tropical climate

Louise Robertson Emmett – Deputy Head Teacher of the Junior School, British School Jakarta, Jakarta, Indonesia

The British School Jakarta (BSJ), Indonesia, formally the British International School Jakarta, was founded in 1973, initially as a primary school in central Jakarta but has since moved to its present location south of Jakarta in 1994. It is a very green site with lots of open spaces and fields. The school itself has grown to its current capacity of 1400 on roll, educating students between the ages of 3-18 years and catering for over 35 different nationalities. The school is very successful with a very popular Early Years Provision and at the other end of the scale excellent attainment at IGCSE, as well as a highly successful International Baccalaureate Diploma sixth form. The Early Years Foundation Stage (EYFS) has an optimum capacity of 120 children, 40 children in Foundation Stage 1 and increasing to 80 children in Foundation Stage 2. In 2009 the school commenced a remodelling in the EYFS of the buildings and facilities. The project was completed January 2010 and opened by the then British Ambassador His Excellency Mark Canning.

The School has an open plan environment covering 1000 square metres indoors and 1755 square meters outdoors. The EYFS Unit has zoned areas for cooking, , art, literacy, imaginative play, gross and fine motor, numeracy and small world - all focusing on skills development. There is also a withdrawal room and storage. All other learning spaces are created in the open plan environment, there are no classrooms enclosed with walls but instead class bases for registration and carpet time. It is very light and airy where glass and mirrors play a huge part in the environment for display, light and imagery. Each class base has an interactive white board at child height. The school is an Apple School so there is Apple TV available in each base. The EYFS Unit is equipped with computers with an allocation of three children to one desktop computer, banks of tablets, android phones and netbooks. Some specialist IT equipment such as listening and recording books have been introduced and these are assigned one child to one recording book. Each class base has an assigned teacher and teaching assistant. There is one additional teaching assistant shared between all teachers across the unit.

The curriculum implemented at the school is predominantly based around the English Early Years Foundation Stage curriculum, but also draws upon good practice from the Northern Irish curriculum, Australia Early Years curriculum and the ethos of Reggio Emilio (Italy). Planning for the learning takes place on a daily basis and plans are created as a collaborative team, this includes all teachers and teaching assistants. Everyone's ideas and opinions are valued and shared. The planning is totally child centred and builds on the interests of the children within topic based planning. The EYFS is totally free flow for the whole day, with the exceptions of regular whole class, group work and independent activities across the week including specialist music, specialist PE and swimming and whole EYFS Unit phonics.

Some of the environmental challenges include the Indonesian climate and the wildlife. The daily temperature is consistently above 30 degrees centigrade all year and there is an approximately five month monsoon season during term time from October to February. The other issue is the wildlife for the outdoor play environment; snakes, rats, musang and mosquitoes. This means that all static outdoor play equipment must be fully checked on a regular basis throughout the day. One of the nastier diseases that cannot be vaccinated against is Dengue Fever. Some of the precautions taken are that mosquito repellent plants are planted both outdoors and in pots near the play areas and electronic mosquito killers are fitted throughout the inside of the building.

The focus on the resources for the outdoor area varies. There are two main pieces of static equipment; these include a climbing frame tower that was relocated during the refurbishment and a very large sand pit. All other equipment is moveable and storable. Much is made out of eco-friendly materials such as bamboo screens and string screens; these do however deteriorate and need to be replaced regularly. Specialist play equipment such as trays for sand, water and, gunk and goo are available, and are renewed on a daily basis. Real life resources such as wood, sticks, leaves, pebbles and soil are constantly used. Tunnels and shapes have been purchased for gross motor development. The school has a cottage garden patch for growing vegetables, flowers and other plants. All aspects of the Early Years Foundation Stage learning goals are addressed and learning opportunities provided and developed.

When the building was redesigned in 2009, all doors to the outdoor environment were replaced with sliding doors so that the free flow curriculum could be facilitated. A complete open sided roof was built to create a fully covered outdoor space for use in all weathers as well as a place for rolling snack. A rolling snack system was introduced once the new facility was opened so that the children can choose to eat their snack whenever they want; they eat when hungry and develop independence for their food and eating habits. Large tarpaulin sails were also fitted so that the grassy areas can be used throughout the day including the hottest part of the day. This can cause issues as the weight of water sitting in the tarpaulins has to be monitored as a matter of health and safety, a slanted static roof would not allow for the free flow of air in tropics based climate. The focus on the space inside is that the walls provide a blank canvas for celebration of children's work, the resources and colour schemes. The furniture is all natural wood and neutral in colour and many of the play resources are imported as they are not manufactured in Indonesia.

The key to such a successful learning environment has been to develop a provision which provides rigorous learning opportunities in a safe and creative, problem solving environment, where risks and exploration can take place. Risk taking opportunities and safe use of equipment and resources are taken into account by all the setting staff.

There is a focus on independence for individual children. This has been particularly important in what has been described as the "Asian nanny culture", where much is completed for the children by the adult carer including feeding and dressing. Nannies are actively discouraged from the EYFS Unit and have had some training in previous years with regard to preparing healthy food and encouraging the child's independence.

Another aspect that was initially a challenge was to overcome the Asian perception of what school and learning looks like, and educating the 'Asian Tiger Mother'. A great deal of work on partnership with parents has been carried out by the Assistant Head and the Early Years Year Leader for the provision. The focus has been on development and learning, strategies to support your child and understanding what happens in school. This has been developed through the following strategies; multimedia blogs, newsletters, leaflets, workshops, coffee mornings, parent drop-ins and parent volunteers. The Assistant Head for this stage of the curriculum at the school has focused a great deal of time and effort into developing parent understanding and cooperation in the partnership of their child's learning.

For the children the key focus is ownership, the children own their learning, they feel confident in their environment and they can learn in a way that best suits them, depending on their age, gender or stage of development. It is a fun environment where the children are constantly engaged and all use the term "Let's get busy".

Support for English as an Additional Language (EAL) has been highlighted as an area of development throughout the school. Therefore robust support and development of speaking and listening activities, drama, role play, immersion in areas of expertise for the child in the role play are part of the practice with younger children. The EYFS Unit is English language rich, with resources and expert English language speaking so for those who have English as a second language, it is total language immersion environment.

How do we know that the provision is successful? There is always anecdotal happy customer feedback but the teachers, involving the teaching assistants, have developed a rigorous assessment procedure for qualitative data gathering, using technology through interactive learning diaries, including photographs, film recording, observations and group focus children. Each child has a key person who is responsible for monitoring all the individual child's early years outcomes, achieved or that need further development. However any adult can make a note of what they have observed. BJS uses a commercial summative data tracking system for this.

For BJS the next steps have been the inclusion of Key Stage 1, Years 1 and 2 in this style and approach to learning. This phase of development uses the International Primary Curriculum (IPC) as its curriculum framework. The development of the outdoor free flow learning environment has already commenced. There has also been a great deal of work on transition from the Early Years Foundation Stage to Key Stage 1. The role of play in effective learning is important at BSJ and so the high quality experience offered to the youngest children are being adapted to support Key Stage 1.

Louise Robertson Emmett

Louise Robertson Emmet has been Deputy Head Teacher at the British School, Jakarta for the past four years. Over the past 18 years she has been instrumental in leading developments in early years practice in schools both in the UK and Asia. She has held two Headships in the UK in primary schools within the maintained sector, a Headship in the independent sector and a Deputy Headship in secondary education. Louise holds a Bachelor of Education degree from Nottingham University and a Masters Degree from Leicester University. She is a mother of three children.

Outdoor learning: back to nature

Chris Hupp, Lower School teacher at ACS Cobham International School in Surrey, UK

Currently 1,500 students from some 70 nationalities attend ACS Cobham, which offers the International Baccalaureate Diploma, College Board Advanced Placement and US Diploma programmes to High School students. Yet, it is the campus itself, surrounded by 120 acres of land, which has encouraged the teaching faculty to become a leader in outdoor education. The school grounds include mature broadleaf and plantation woodlands; open meadows; extensive sports facilities and landscaped grounds as well as a pond and bird-hide, river access, wetland, nature trails, various outdoor classroom structures, and a large vegetable garden.

Embedding outdoor education into the curriculum is not without its challenges. Predominantly, helping key stakeholders - teachers, parents and students - in a transient international environment to understand the benefits and efficiently integrating outdoor learning across the curriculum. At ACS learning outdoors is a thread running through all stages of the education we offer. Our aim is to not simply improve what we already do or just restructure the responsibility for outdoor education in the classroom, what Sterling (2001) calls the 'first order of change'. We strive to achieve the second and third order of change, that is 'doing better things' and 'seeing things differently', ultimately a fundamental shift in our education paradigm which places outdoor education at the heart of the curriculum.

Our approach...

Our vision, *Through learning inspire all to make a difference* is the cornerstone to the ACS school philosophy. This statement provides a powerful framework for envisioning teaching and learning at our school and a way for outdoor education to emerge naturally in our teaching practices. This statement represents three foundational areas of teaching and learning: *academic growth* (Through learning...), *social-emotional development (...*inspire all...) and *global citizenship* (...to make a difference.). All of these are as relevant to young learners as to the older students of the school.

This triad reflects our core beliefs, which see learning as an active process of exploration in a collaborative environment with positive social relationships, rather than a merely passive and transactional educational experience. The learning triad provides a multi-hued spectrum of experience, a complete *learner profile,* providing authentic and transformative teaching and learning, which gives rise to healthier, more fulfilling, and more sustainable ways of living for our students and ourselves.

It finally reflects the awareness that the ultimate outcomes of learning should lead us toward positive change in the world through service and constructive social action. The student who emerges is truly a global citizen and life-long learner, with the knowledge and deep understanding that allows them to work and act in ways that leave the world a better place.

We believe that outdoor learning is an ideal platform from which students can and should deeply engage in their learning in these three interconnected domains, which can equally be understood as the relationship between *head* (thinking), *heart* (feeling), and hands (*doing*).

Through learning...

Academic growth, in the context of outdoor learning, refers to the ways we can enrich knowledge acquisition through experience and self-discovery. From this perspective, we are beginning to understand at ACS that knowledge in and of itself is more of an approximation and abstraction; learning outside the classroom allows us to *verify* what we know through living experience and practical research. Only once we have explored and discovered truth for ourselves are we able to apply and synthesise learning in truly creative ways. This is a self-discovery which comes about through the fostering of natural curiosity about the world and providing hands-on learning situations that give students topics that are important to think and talk about, ample time to experiment and explore, and plenty of opportunities to make sense of their observations.

A recent case study from our 3rd grade (eight/nine year olds) team demonstrates how this dynamic approach can emerge out of commitment to more integrated and hands-on learning with strong connections to outdoor learning. The team redesigned a social studies unit on Native Americans for their students. The unit involved traditional storytelling under the Tom Tent, a large teepee set in the school's woodlands. Students sat around a fire on several occasions and listened to ancient legends. The smell of traditional sweet grass incense, the natural rhythm of drums, and the bird-like voice of a Native American flute all worked to deepen learning and add a rich layer from which student understanding began to grow.

Each story was connected to core concepts taught in the unit revolving around the idea of indigenous culture, such as family relationships, belief in the sacredness of the natural world, or the skills needed for survival. These ideas were explored further through song and traditional crafts including sewing, painting, and the making of dream-catchers.

Forest School sessions explored a variety of Native American skills such as methods for constructing shelters, animal tracking, and games or sports that trained young warriors. These lessons powerfully laid the groundwork for academic learning in the classroom. Students became highly engaged and self-motivated, often spending time outside of school learning about Native Americans simply because they wanted to. As part of a culminating learning experience, students chose a research topic that connected to their own personal interests. They each developed a research question related to the concepts studied: What sports did Native peoples play? Who were the doctors in tribes? What shelter had the strongest structure?"

While this case study does not necessarily represent all learning that takes place throughout the school, it does demonstrate a growing belief that outdoor learning can bring deeper learning to classrooms. It is possible for schools to achieve a more transdisciplinary approach in which various subject areas overlap in dynamic and organic ways. This is essentially a movement toward an ecological metaphor, which views life as a series of interconnected and interpenetrating systems.

The learning system is not, ecologically speaking, a set of discrete and separated subjects. It is rather a rich melody of knowledge, experience, and language that brings us into dynamic relation to the deeper mystery of a complex, multi-faceted natural and human world. At ACS we have the significant challenge of familiarising our community with the idea that knowledge and learning can be interconnected and cut across disciplines, rather than an isolated and fractured subject area approach that tends to dominate our current methodology.

...inspire all...

Social-Emotional Development refers to the values, attitudes, and inter-personal skills we hope to instill in learners and is best understood by its focus on personal inspiration, empathy for all life, positive feelings toward challenge and risk, and a life-long sympathy for learning. We believe that outdoor learning provides us with a unique platform, an entire living landscape, from which students can develop these fundamental qualities which make them productive life-long learners.

Outdoor learning allows us to participate more fully with others, entering into deeper and more fulfilling interpersonal relationships in communion with a living world. With an emphasis on place, outdoor education roots positive learning experiences in the land and encourages children and families to explore beyond buildings and get out into the natural world. This gives rise to healthier living and mindsets, which feed back in a positive way to greater capacity for and interest in learning.

At ACS we offer a wide variety of outdoor activities which aim at developing a social-emotional foundation for learning, from performing arts, bush craft experiences, field trips, and much more. However, we have adopted three well-developed and research-backed approaches, which are beginning to give significant shape and purpose to the social-emotional curriculum at the school. Responsive Classroom, Forest Schools, and Outward-Bound are examples of approaches that use fun, risk, and empathy as the foundational design principles that are the basis for academic achievement. They provide teaching models that allow teachers to usher children into more fulfilling relationships, more positive self-image and esteem, greater confidence and leadership, and stronger communication and collaboration.

This year two 1st grade classes (aged four/five) have committed to going outside on a weekly basis to help teach children how to observe their world, communicate with others their ideas about their observations, and work together to achieve challenging design tasks set for them. While the activities they explore have connections to classroom learning, the aims of this activity are have around social-emotional learning and developing self-management, relationship skills and responsible decision-making.

Students recently studied artworks by Andrew Goldsworthy discussing various elements in class such as gradation, hue, and form. In groups, students then selected which art task they would recreate outdoors and reflect on their experience asking such questions as *What was a challenge or obstacle? How did you overcome these obstacles? What worked well for your team?* These types of questions promote self-awareness and lead to more effective relationships with other children. Both 1st grade teachers noted that these skills have easily transferred to classroom tasks, with students more focused, able to work productively in learning activities and reflect on the challenges and success of their work.

...to make a difference.
The global citizenship lens puts learning into the perspective of local, regional, and global concerns. Here the focus is on bringing about positive change in an increasingly complex and interconnected world through service, leadership, and meaningful social action. This domain is the culmination of academic learning and social-emotional development. Acquisition of diverse knowledge in fields such as ecology, economics, languages, political systems, and culture combined with a sense of empathy and compassion form the foundation for becoming positive agents for change in the world. Here we are speaking of a truly cross-disciplinary approach, which fully integrates the *thinking, feeling,* and *doing* triad.

Fieldwork and service-learning, in the context of outdoor learning, is the principal way we can prepare children for growing into successful global citizens. In contrast to traditional field trips in which the learner tends to be a passive participant, fieldwork provides children with opportunities to develop leadership skills and transdisciplinary knowledge. Fieldwork allows students to actively apply their learning while grappling with complex problems facing the world today: climate change and species extinction, growing poverty and structures of economic inequities, and increased violence and terrorism, to name a few. In this way, global citizenship is very much related to environmental stewardship and social justice, despite being what are often considered inconvenient (albeit undeniable) demands of our current age.

One recent fieldwork example has emerged from a middle school science class studying local environmental issues. The elective course set out to study the unique ecology of the Mole River, which borders the northern edge of the campus. The river flows through a number of commercial, industrial, residential, and agricultural sites on its way to the Thames. The science teacher felt this was an authentic learning experience and so designed a number of lessons that incorporated a variety of skills including geography, chemistry, biology, mathematics, and writing. Lessons in class explored the connections between these fields in relation to the unique features of the river.

Every third lesson happened outdoors, with data collecting expeditions to the river. On one of their expeditions, the students found a strange substance oozing into the river from nearby farmland. This discovery sparked a host of questions from students and led to a real-to-life enquiry around the issues of pollution and farming practices. Local scientific experts were invited to join the class on their learning journey, offering students insight into the real work that professionals carry out in and around our communities. In a sense the learning has taken on a life of its own, leading the class toward deeper and more authentic learning.

While service-learning was initially not an explicit outcome of the course, the opportunity to engage pupils in meaningful action caused the course to morph throughout the unit of study; students are now being challenged to find ways to engage their local community through raising awareness about pollution and providing a range of creative solutions.

Students at ACS also learn to shape their world through activities that support real-world application, individual self-determination, and participation in local, regional, and global movements for change. The Duke of Edinburgh Awards, Namibia Project, and the Boy and Girl Scout communities are excellent examples of how ACS students are already working for positive change through leadership and compassion.

Moving forward...

At ACS there is still work to be done to help our community understand the new vision of education that outdoor learning can bring to international schools. We have taken the first steps toward significant change as we integrate outdoor learning into academic and social learning in ways that are more efficient and effective. Providing teachers with training and online resources has formed an important part of this ongoing approach. We have also worked to minimise red tape with risk assessments and have carefully developed the grounds, making them more accessible and safe for teachers and pupils.

The creation of a more coherent and comprehensive service-learning curriculum is a key long-term development goal for our outdoor programme at ACS. The school has great potential to lead the way in outdoor education through fieldwork and experience based learning which connects to local and global issues. These principles are, after all, already reflected in our core values of developing global citizens and preparing students for the challenges and opportunities of the 21st century. The increasing pressures and difficulties faced on both local and global levels make this *the* educational imperative of our time.

References

Sterling, S. (2001). *Sustainable Education: Revisioning Learning and Change (Schumacher Briefings)*, Jan 2001

Chris Hupp

Chris Hupp is a Lower School teacher at ACS Cobham International School in Surrey, UK. He has a particular interest in learning outdoors and shares this with pupils across the key stages at ACS - sometimes using the extensive grounds of the school and sometimes at other locations.